But God Says

Deborah Lynne

Let Him have the final Word in your life!

Copyright

Dedication

I dedicate this book to God as I share Him with everyone who reads what He laid on my heart to share.

Remember, God loves us and never leaves us.

We are who God Says we are, But we have to walk in our faith in Him and our faith in His Word, trusting, resting and believing Him...what God Says in His Word, in the Holy Bible.

I pray after reading this book, you dig deeper into the Holy Bible and know He is talking to all of you who accept Him as your Savior...and I believe that is you.

God bless you!

Scripture

Hebrews 10:14 - For by that one offering He forever made perfect those who are being made holy.

God's will is for us to be made holy by the sacrifice of Jesus Christ, His Son. He did this for us because He loves us. And once we accept Him as our Savior, we are covered in Jesus' blood and made perfect in God's sight. Praise God!

Introduction

We have a bad habit of saying the first thing that comes to our mind. What we need to understand is that what we speak out loud can delay the plans God has for each of us. We need to read His Word and learn what He tells us in His Word—focus on the truth—His Word.

We need to <u>know</u> God spoke good over His people.

He has great plans for each of us. We, as believers, need to stay in His Word focused on what He Says about us, about our lives—then watch what we say.

We live tomorrow what we speak today. If you don't believe it, try thinking about the words that came out of your mouth a day or so ago, or even a week, a month, a year ago. Did you speak good things and good things are coming your way? God's plan for each of us is good. Or have you been speaking bad things and are living them now. Don't get me wrong. Bad things, troublesome things, come into our lives. God told us so. But you don't want to add bad that wasn't part of your walk. Pay attention to what you say. Watch how you speak. Try to be so filled with His Word that you can't help But speak blessings over you, your family, and your friends...strangers as well.

Are you speaking the words God has spoken over you? Great if you are. You are keeping the well open for Him to pour down the blessings He wants on you. Don't clog them up. Stay in His Word. Speak favor over you and your family and friends.

Know that God is love. He speaks good over us, But we must believe it and walk in it while speaking in <u>agreement</u> with Him and His Word.

In this book, God has led me to share with you the good things He speaks over us—all His believers and followers. We need to speak in agreement with Him. We also need to remember we have to be consistent in our belief in His Word, consistently speaking His truth.

In the beginning, I will mention something we may say or think about our lives under "We Say" in quotes, and then I will say also in quotes after "But God Says," what God Says to me/you about that very thing in His Word, paraphrasing, by me, with His guidance, His Word as if God is speaking in response to "We say" in today speak, and then I will back what I say "But God Says" with **His Word**.

Know that it's up to you to turn your life around. It's your faith in Him and His Word that will turn your sorrows into joy. Start living and thinking on purpose. Don't let your mouth override the great plans God has for you.

I hope you'll take His Words to heart and know God loves you and wants the best for you. I pray after reading this short book, you will think twice about the words you let fall out of your mouth.

God bless you.

One more thing...in the end He has encouraged me to share what I say aloud, words He's led me to speak over my life, declarations I speak over myself, after telling me these things in His Word that I read daily. I'd love to say I speak them daily. Some I do. Some I don't. But know this is my version of like when Jesus was tempted by Satan in Matthew 4:1-11. He used God's Word to stand against Satan — As it is written. The truth of God's Word can help you through anything in your life. You just have to take time to familiarize yourself with God's Word...The Holy Bible.

I speak what I've written aloud, promises and blessings I've received from Him through His Word. I hope you'll make your own list. You are welcome to use any or all of mine.

Again, what I say on these final pages, is a list of things I speak over me that I've gathered from Scripture. I suggest you find His Words that speak to you and you write them down and then speak them over yourself...letting His Word be your strength and direction daily.

We say - "I can't go on."

But God Says - "You can live another day. Your life isn't over. I have great plans for you. My Spirit lives in you. And just as I raised Christ Jesus from the dead, I will give life to your mortal body by My Spirit living in you."

Jeremiah 29:11 - *For I know the plans I have for you," Says the LORD. "They are plans for good and not for disaster, to give you a future and a hope...."*

Romans 8:11 - *The Spirit of God, who raised Jesus from the dead, lives in you. And just as God raised Christ Jesus from the dead, He will give life to your mortal bodies by this same Spirit living within you.*

We say - "I'm a failure!"

But God Says - "You are not perfect. But I promise I will always be here for you. And if you turn to me in your times of trouble or failure, I will lift you back up. I love you and will never give up on you. But you have to believe in Me and believe in yourself."

Deuteronomy 31:6 - *So be strong and courageous! Do not be afraid and do not panic before them. For the LORD your God will personally go ahead of you. He will neither fail you nor abandon you.*

Proverbs 24:16 - *The Godly may trip seven times, But they will get up again. But one disaster is enough to overthrow the wicked.*

We say - "I can't help myself. I'm so tempted. I can't resist."

But God Says - "I promise to always help you out of temptation, if you will listen to Me and follow My plans for you."

1 Corinthians 10:13 - *The temptations in your life are no different from what others experience. And God is faithful. He will not allow the temptation to be more than you can stand. When you are tempted, He will show you a way out so that you can endure.*

We say - "I got laid off. I'm too old to start another career, or a new job. Who will hire me at my age? I don't know how I'm going to take care of my family."

But God Says - "I am your provider. Do not worry."

Matthew 6:25-26 - *"That is why I tell you not to worry about everyday life—whether you have enough food and drink, or enough clothes to wear. Isn't life more than food, and your body more than clothing. Look at the birds. They don't plant or harvest or store food in barns, for your heavenly Father feeds them. And aren't you far more valuable to Him than they are?"*

We say - "Why can't I ever get ahead? There's never enough money to do anything extra."

But God Says - "I supply all your needs and give you the desires of your heart, But you must do your part. Keep My Word in your heart. Speak it in belief over and over believing what I tell you. And most of all, live it!"

Joshua 1:8 - *Study this Book of Instruction continually. Meditate on it day and night so you will be sure to obey everything written in it. Only then will you prosper and succeed in all you do.*

We say - "These allergies are killing me. Why do I always get this sinus infection?"

But God Says - "I am your healer. Ask Me and trust Me to do what I say. Don't speak death over you, and definitely don't commit to getting sick over and over. Watch what you say. That is not my plan for you."

Jeremiah 17:14 - *O LORD, if You heal me, I will be truly healed; if You save me, I will be truly saved. My praises are for You alone!*

Jeremiah 30:17 - *"...I will give you back your health and heal your wounds," Says the LORD. "For you are called an outcast—'Jerusalem for whom no one cares.'"*

Matthew 12:37 - *"The words you say will either acquit you or condemn you."*

We say - "I feel so alone. No one seems to be listening to me. No one hears my cry for help."

But God Says - "I hear you. Talk to Me. I am always listening to you, and I am always present with you."

Psalm 23:6 - *Surely Your goodness and unfailing love will pursue me all the days of my life, and I will live in the house of the LORD forever.*

We say - "I'm being pulled every direction...my family, my church, my friends, my job. There's not enough time in the day to please everyone."

But God Says - "I am your shepherd...Let Me lead you. It appears you are saying yes to everything. That is not my plan for you. Ask me what you should do. Let me lead you and you will find rest and joy in your life."

Psalm 23:1-2 - *The LORD is my shepherd; I have all that I need. He lets me rest in green meadows; He leads me beside peaceful streams.*

We say - "My world has turned upside down. My job is having lay-offs...and that might include me. What am I going to do?"

But God Says - "Give your problems to Me. Let Me help you, and I will give you peace."

Matthew 11:28-30 - *Then Jesus said, "Come to Me, all of you who are weary and carry heavy burdens, and I will give you rest. Take My yoke upon you. Let Me teach you, because I am humble and gentle at heart, and you will find rest for your souls. For My yoke is easy to bear, and the burden I give you is light."*

We say - "I'm so tired of being alone. No one loves me."

But God Says - "I am here for you. Turn to me. I love you, child of Mine."

John 15:9 - "I have loved you even as the Father has loved Me. Remain in My love...."

We say - "I do so much for the church. Why is it never enough?"

But God Says - "Are you working for them? Or are you working for Me? Your faith in Me is all you need, if you are working for Me. If you are working for man, then you will get what you get in that moment, and then they will probably ask for more. But with Me your faith, not your work, is what I want. Your faith in Me lets Me forgive you; saves you...makes you righteous. Let Me lead you, not man. You can tell them no. You don't have to do everything man asks. Trust Me. Follow My lead."

Psalm 27:1 - *The LORD is my light and my salvation—so why should I be afraid? The LORD is my fortress, protecting me from danger, so why should I tremble.*

Proverbs 3:5-6 - *Trust in the LORD with all your heart; do not depend on your own understanding. Seek His will in all you do, and He will show you which path to take.*

Isaiah 51:12 - *"I, yes I, am the One who comforts you. So why are you afraid of mere humans, who wither like the grass and disappear?..."*

Jeremiah 17:5 - *This is what the LORD Says: "Cursed are those who put their trust in mere humans, who rely on human strength and turn their hearts away from the LORD."*

Romans 4:5 - *But people are counted as righteous, not because of their work, But because of their faith in God who forgives sinners.*

We say - "Everything I try to do, I fail at it. Why me?"

But God Says - "Things go wrong in this world, But if you'll turn to Me and trust Me, I will bring good through your issues of life...make good from the bad that is surrounding you. But you must lean on Me, trust Me, and follow My Word."

Psalm 73:26 - *My health may fail, and my spirit may grow weak, But God remains the strength of my heart; He is mine forever.*

Romans 8:28 - *And we know that God causes everything to work together for the good of those who love God and are called according to His purpose for them.*

2 Corinthians 12:9-10 - *Each time He said, "My grace is all you need. My power works best in weakness." So now I am glad to boast about my weaknesses, so that the power of Christ can work through me.*

We say - "Jim is so lucky. Why does everything good happen to him? What about me? Can't I get a little of that luck too?"

But God Says - "I want to bless you. This is My desire. But you must read My Word, believe it, and live it. I want to bless you in abundance."

Deuteronomy 28:2 - *You will experience all these blessings if you obey the LORD your God:...*

John 10:10 - *The thief's purpose is to steal and kill and destroy. My purpose is to give them a rich and satisfying life.*

Romans 8:32 - *Since He did not spare even His own Son But gave Him up for us all, won't He also give us everything else?*

We say - "I knew this was going to be a horrible day. I told my husband things were going bad at work and would only get worse. I knew it! I knew it!"

But God Says - "My dear. You also said it over and over. I wanted to help make things right for you, But you kept on saying how bad things were going and how worse they were going to get. Read My Word. You get what you speak, so watch what you say and how you speak it. Instead of thinking and speaking the worst, pray and ask Me for the best. If you do, I will turn things around for you."

Proverbs 21:23 - *Watch your tongue and keep your mouth shut, and you will stay out of trouble.*

Matthew 12:37 - *"The words you say will either acquit you or condemn you."*

John 14:13-14 - *"You can ask for anything in My name, and I will do it, so that the Son can bring glory to the Father. Yes, ask Me for anything in My name, and I will do it!"*

We say - "The world is going to hell in a hand basket. That's all you hear about on the news and read in the newspapers. They must know exactly what is going on. How am I going to make it? How will I keep my family fed and clothed...and in our home."

But God Says - "If you'll put your trust in Me instead of the world news, I will get you through it all. I will protect you, But you must trust in Me and on Me. As a believer you should rely on Me and what My Word tells you. Seek My Kingdom and live righteously. I'll give you what you need. Put your trust in Me."

Nahum 1:7 - *The LORD is good, a strong refuge when trouble comes. He is close to those who trust in Him.*

Matthew 6:31-33 - *"So don't worry about these things, saying, 'What will we eat? What will we drink? What will we wear?' These things dominate the thoughts of unbelievers, But your heavenly Father already knows all your needs. Seek the Kingdom of God above all else, and live righteously, and He will give you everything you need."*

1 Timothy 6:17 - *Teach those who are rich in this world not to be proud and not to trust in their money, which is so unreliable. Their trust should be in God, who richly gives us all we need for our enjoyment.*

We say - "I can't do this. I'm not strong enough."

But God Says - "You can do it. I am your strength, and I give strength to you. You who are My children, run to Me. Lean on Me. Trust in Me. With Me you can do anything. And I am always here for you."

Nehemiah 8:10 - *And Nehemiah continued, "Go and celebrate with a feast of rich foods and sweet drinks, and share gifts of food with people who have nothing prepared. This is a sacred day before our Lord. Don't be dejected and sad, for the joy of the LORD is your strength!"*

Psalm 46:1 - *God is our refuge and strength, always ready to help in times of trouble.*

Proverbs 18:10 - *The name of the LORD is a strong fortress; the Godly run to Him and are safe.*

Philippians 4:13 - *For I can do everything through Christ, who gives me strength.*

We say - "Does anybody really care about me?"

But God Says - "I care. I tell you to give Me all of your problems and I'll take care of them for you. But you have to let go and let Me do what's right for you. I even call you by name. You are a child of Mine for your whole lifetime once you invite Me in, But then again, you have to let go and put your faith in Me to do what is best for you. I want to bless you. Let Me, please."

Psalm 55:22 - *Give your burdens to the LORD, and He will take care of you. He will not permit the Godly to slip and fall.*

Isaiah 46:4 - *I will be your God throughout your lifetime—until your hair is white with age. I made you, and I will care for you. I will carry you along and save you.*

John 10:3, 6-7 - *The gatekeeper opens the gate for him, and the sheep recognize his voice and come to him. He calls His own sheep by name and leads them out.... Those who heard Jesus use this illustration didn't understand what He meant, so he explained it to them: "I tell you the truth, I am the gate for the sheep....*

1 Peter 5:7 - *Give all your worries and cares to God, for He cares about you.*

1 John 4:9 - *God showed how much He loved us by sending His one and only Son into the world so that we might have eternal life through Him.*

We say - "I really thought this new job would fix all my problems. Why is there never enough?"

But God Says - "Because you put your faith in your new job. Try putting your faith in Me. Even the smallest amount of faith in Me and My Word will turn your life around."

Psalm 33:20 - *We put our hope in the LORD. He is our help and our shield.*

Psalm 37:4-5 - *Take delight in the LORD, and He will give you your heart's desires. Commit everything you do to the LORD. Trust Him, and He will help you.*

Proverbs 3:5-6 - *Trust in the LORD with all your heart; do not depend on your own understanding. Seek His will in all you do, and He will show you which path to take.*

Matthew 17:20 - *"You don't have enough faith," Jesus told them. "I tell you the truth, if you had faith even as small as a mustard seed, you could say to this mountain, 'Move from here to there,' and it would move. Nothing would be impossible."*

We say - "How can I resist this urge that keeps coming over me?"

But God Says - **"Resist the devil by using My Word. I give you strength and courage through My Word. Use it. Put it into practice."**

Matthew 26:41 - *"Keep watch and pray, so that you will not give in to temptation. For the spirit is willing, But the body is weak!"*

1 Corinthians 10:13 - *The temptations in your life are no different from what others experience. And God is faithful. He will not allow the temptation to be more than you can stand. When you are tempted, He will show you a way out so that you can endure.*

Ephesians 6:17 - *Put on salvation as your helmet, and take the sword of the Spirit, which is the Word of God.*

James 4:7 - *So humble yourselves before God. Resist the devil, and he will flee from you.*

1 Peter 5:8-9 - *Stay alert! Watch out for your great enemy, the devil. He prowls around like a roaring lion, looking for someone to devour. Stand firm against him, and be strong in your faith. Remember that your family of believers all over the world is going through the same kind of suffering you are.*

We say - "My poor child. Why isn't his life better than it is. I know he knows You, Lord. But things are not going right for him. He is not living in Your blessings What have we done wrong? I know we raised all of our children in the Lord and each one accepted You as their Savior."

But God Says - "Trust in Me. Trust in My word. When you teach your children of Me and they find their way in Me, My spirit is in them as well. I tell you so. Staying sinless is impossible with man, that is why I, Jesus, came so that My blood covers all believers. So when a child or a friend is stepping out of God's will, pray for them. Help your child through prayers, opening their eyes wider to Me, Jesus, their Savior. You, parents, keep your faith in Me and My Word, praying for your child to take any blinders off and binding Satan and his cohorts off of your child's life. Be diligent. Pray consistently. Keep shining God's light through you on them."

Proverbs 22:6 - Direct your children onto the right path, and when they are older, they will not leave it.

Isaiah 54:13 - I will teach all your children, and they will enjoy great peace.

Romans 8:15-16 - So you have not received a spirit that makes you fearful slaves. Instead, you received God's Spirit when He adopted you as His own children. Now we call Him, "Abba, Father." For His Spirit joins with our spirit to affirm that we are God's children.

1 John 3:9 - Those who have been born into God's family do not make a practice of sinning, because God's life is in them. So they can't keep on sinning, because they are children of God.

We say - "I know the plans God had for me. He told me what to do and showed me how to do it. Although I'm a lot farther along today than I was when He first led me on His will for me, I don't feel I've accomplished all I should. No where near, in fact. What am I doing wrong? Where did I step off the path He had me on. What do I do now?"

But God Says - "Yes, My dear child. You heard me correctly. Sometimes you get a little impatient. Wait on me. And when you move forward a bit and stop a bit, don't give up. My plan is what I gave you. I am using you in a mighty way. Stay in My peace no matter what comes your way — through the trials, hardships, sorrows, and problems. My grace is all you need. Know I have overcome the world. And through your weakness My strength will prevail."

Matthew 11:28 - *Then Jesus said, "Come to Me, all of you who are weary and carry heavy burdens, and I will give you rest."*

John 16:33 - *"I have told you all this so that you may have peace in Me. Here on earth you will have many trials and sorrows. But take heart, because I have overcome the world."*

2 Corinthians 12:9 - *Each time He said, "My grace is all you need. My power works best in weakness." So now I am glad to boast about my weaknesses, so that the power of Christ can work through me.*

Hebrews 4:16 - *So let us come boldly to the throne of our gracious God. There we will receive His mercy, and we will find grace to help us when we need it most.*

Hebrews 12:2-3 - *We do this by keeping our eyes on Jesus, the champion who initiates and perfects our faith.*

Because of the joy awaiting Him, He endured the cross, disregarding its shame. Now He is seated in the place of honor beside God's throne. Think of all the hostility He endured from sinful people; then you won't become weary and give up.

We say - "I can't go on."

But God Says - "Yes you can. Know that I am here with you and will help you through. Don't ever get tired of moving forward. Know that I am your strength. Do good as you move forward. Just at the right time, My time, you will reap My blessings. Don't ever give up. Never, ever get tired of doing good…that is doing what My Word tells you to do. And be patient while you walk in My will and know that you will receive all that I have promised. You are My child, a child of the Most High God, and I love you truly."

Exodus 15:2 - *The Lord is my strength and my song; He has given me victory. This is my God, and I will praise Him—my Father's God, and I will exalt Him!*

Galatians 3:26 - *For you are all children of God through faith in Christ Jesus.*

Galatians 6:9 - *So let's not get tired of doing what is good. At just the right time we will reap a harvest of blessing if we don't give up.*

2 Thessalonians 3:13 - *As for the rest of you, dear brothers and sisters, never get tired of doing good.*

Hebrews 10:36 - *Patient endurance is what you need now, so that you will continue to do God's will. Then you will receive all that He has promised.*

We say - "What am I doing? I am a piece of wasted space. I've accomplished nothing. My family is better off with out me."

But God Says - "No you are not. Your life isn't over. I have great plans for you. I will show you the way. Take delight in Me and My Word. I don't bring you disaster...Satan does that. Avoid him by staying in Me. My Spirit lives in you. And just as I raised Christ Jesus from the dead, I will give life to your mortal body by My Spirit living in you. So don't worry about tomorrow. Live in today. Work for Me willingly and I will give you the strength you need."

Psalm 16:11 - *You will show me the way of life, granting me the joy of Your presence and the pleasures of living with You forever.*

Psalm 37:4 - *Take delight in the LORD, and He will give you your heart's desires.*

Jeremiah 29:11 - *"For I know the plans I have for you," Says the LORD. "They are plans for good and not for disaster, to give you a future and a hope...."*

Matthew 6:34 - *"So don't worry about tomorrow, for tomorrow will bring its own worries. Today's trouble is enough for today."*

John 10:10 - *The thief's purpose is to steal and kill and destroy. My purpose is to give them a rich and satisfying life.*

Romans 8:11 - *The Spirit of God, who raised Jesus from the dead, lives in you. And just as God raised Christ Jesus from the dead, He will give life to your mortal bodies by this same Spirit living within you.*

Colossians 3:23 - *Work willingly at whatever you do, as though you were working for the Lord rather than for people.*

We say - "I am a failure!"

But God Says - "That is your fear talking. You are not a failure unless you decide to quit. Who are you looking to in order to decide if you are succeeding or not? Surely, not your fellow man. Put your trust in Me. When you rely on others, you will be cursed. This I told you long ago in My Word. Trust in Me and I will bless you. Live as My Word tells you to live and not only will you be blessed, But those around you will want what you have, and you will lead them to Me...bearing fruit...being a success, as I define it."

Psalm 56:3 - *But when I am afraid, I will put my trust in You.*

Jeremiah 17:5-7 - *This is what the LORD Says: "Cursed are those who put their trust in mere humans, who rely on human strength and turn their hearts away from the LORD. They are like stunted shrubs in the desert, with no hope for the future. They will live in the barren wilderness, in an uninhabited salty land. But blessed are those who trust in the LORD and have made the LORD their hope and confidence. They are like trees planted along a riverbank, with roots that reach deep into the water. Such trees are not bothered by the heat or worried by long months of drought. Their leaves stay green, and they never stop producing fruit.*

1 Thessalonians 4:11-12 - *Make it your goal to live a quiet life, minding your own business and working with your hands, just as we instructed you before. Then people who are not believers will respect the way you live, and you will not need to depend on others.*

We say - "Bills, bills, and more bills. How will we ever make ends meet?"

But God Says - "I will help you, But you must listen to Me. Follow My lead."

Psalm 33:20 - *We put our hope in the LORD. He is our help and our shield.*

Psalm 37:25 - *Once I was young, and now I am old. Yet I have never seen the Godly abandoned or their children begging for bread.*

Psalm 91:14-15 - *The LORD Says, "I will rescue those who love Me. I will protect those who trust in My name. When they call on Me, I will answer; I will be with them in trouble. I will rescue and honor them.*

Matthew 6:34 - *"So don't worry about tomorrow, for tomorrow will bring its own worries. Today's trouble is enough for today."*

2 Corinthians 9:8 - *And God will generously provide all you need. Then you will always have everything you need and plenty left over to share with others.*

Philippians 4:6 - *Don't worry about anything; instead, pray about everything. Tell God what you need, and thank Him for all He has done.*

Philippians 4:19 - *And this same God who takes care of me will supply all your needs from His glorious riches, which have been given to us in Christ Jesus.*

We say - "I know what I am supposed to do next. But I don't know if I can. My family lives far away from me. I am so alone. Help me."

But God Says - "You are not alone. I am here with you. I will never leave you or forsake you. What I send you to do, know I am with you. In fact, I go before you making your way. Trust Me. Rest in Me. I will not fail you."

Deuteronomy 31:8 - "Do not be afraid or discouraged, for the LORD will personally go ahead of you. He will be with you; He will neither fail you nor abandon you."

Matthew 28:20b - "...And be sure of this: I am with you always, even to the end of the age."

Philippians 4:19 - And this same God who takes care of me will supply all your needs from His glorious riches, which have been given to us in Christ Jesus.

We say - "Most of my adult life, I've trusted you. Lately, I feel I've made so many mistakes. Why would you still try to help me make good out of my life. I seem to mess up every day. In fact, if there is one thing lately I know I can count on, it's me screwing up. How do I fix this?"

But God Says - "First off, you have to let Me fix it. You tell Me you've messed up and want My help to fix you, and I will. But you have to acknowledge your need of Me. I'm here for you every day. Relax, rest, and trust Me."

Exodus 14:14 - "*The LORD Himself will fight for you. Just stay calm.*"

Isaiah 41:10 - *Don't be afraid, for I am with you. Don't be discouraged, for I am your God. I will strengthen you and help you. I will hold you up with My victorious right hand.*

Lamentations 3:22-23 - *The faithful love of the LORD never ends! His mercies never cease. Great is His faithfulness; His mercies begin afresh each morning.*

Matthew 11:28 - *Then Jesus said, "Come to Me, all of you who are weary and carry heavy burdens, and I will give you rest...."*

Philippians 4:19 - *And this same God who takes care of me will supply all your needs from His glorious riches, which have been given to us in Christ Jesus.*

We say - "I am so alone. My husband has passed away, my kids are all grown up. It's just me. What can I do?"

But God Says - "Stay in Me. If you will stay close to Me, I'll stay with you. I'll be your strength. I'll give you victory. Don't be sad. You are not alone. I am with you! Lean on Me and trust Me, and I will get you through everything that comes your way."

Exodus 15:2 - The LORD is my strength and my song; He has given me victory. This is my God, and I will praise Him—my father's God, and I will exalt Him!

Nehemiah 8:10b - "...Don't be dejected and sad, for the joy of the LORD is your strength!"

Isaiah 41:10 - "Don't be afraid, for I am with you. Don't be discouraged, for I am your God. I will strengthen you and help you. I will hold you up with My victorious right hand.

John 15:5 - "Yes, I am the vine; you are the branches. Those who remain in Me, and I in them, will produce much fruit. For apart from Me you can do nothing...."

We say - "The storm is coming. Everyone Says it's going to be bad, especially the weather reporters. I'm confused and a little anxious. What should I do?"

But God Says - "Follow My plans for you and I will be with you through it all. I'll be your strength. Celebrate the life I give you and know I will cover you and keep you safe...as long as your trust is totally in Me. I'll help you through the bad times...stay close to Me. Abide in Me and know I'll see you through."

Exodus 15:2 - The LORD is my strength and my song: He has given me victory. This is my God, and I will praise Him—my father's God, and I will exalt Him!

Exodus 33:14 - The LORD replied, "I will personally go with you, Moses, and I will give you rest—everything will be fine for you."

Nehemiah 8:10 - And Nehemiah continued, "Go and celebrate with a feast of rich foods and sweet drinks, and share gifts of food with people who have nothing prepared. This is a sacred day before our Lord. Don't be dejected and sad, for the joy of the LORD is your strength!"

Psalm 46:1-3 - God is our refuge and strength, always ready to help in times of trouble. So we will not fear when earthquakes come and the mountains crumble into the sea. Let the oceans roar and foam. Let the mountains tremble as the waters surge!

Proverbs 18:10 - The name of the LORD is a strong fortress; the Godly run to Him and are safe.

Isaiah 41:10 - Don't be afraid, for I am with you. Don't be discouraged, for I am your God. I will strengthen you and help you. I will hold you up with My victorious right hand.

We say - "There is never enough time in the day for all I have to do, between work, family, life, and doing for You, God. It's so unfair. So stressful trying to get everything done that I have to do."

But God Says - "Put me first!!! Rest in Me and do what I lead you to do. Seek Me and My Word, living the life I've planned for you, and I will give you everything you need. Don't follow the world and try to have what your neighbor might have. I may have something even better for you, But you must trust in Me and put Me first."

Psalm 37:5 - *Commit everything you do to the LORD. Trust Him, and He will help you.*

Proverbs 23:4 - *Don't wear yourself out trying to get rich. Be wise enough to know when to quit.*

Matthew 6:33 - *Seek the Kingdom of God above all else, and live righteously, and He will give you everything you need.*

Luke 10:41-42 - *But the Lord said to her, "My dear Martha, you are worried and upset over all these details! There is only one thing worth being concerned about. Mary has discovered it, and it will not be taken away from her."*

Luke 12:25 - *Can all your worries add a single moment to your life?*

Romans 12:2 - *Don't copy the behavior and customs of this world, But let God transform you into a new person by changing the way you think. Then you will learn to know God's will for you, which is good and pleasing and perfect.*

James 1:12 - *God blesses those who patiently endure testing and temptation. Afterward they will receive the crown of life that God has promised to those who love Him.*

We say - "How can I know my faith is real? Show me, please."

But God Says - "If your faith is in Me, you must believe I exist and reward those who believe in Me. We will be friends, as you abide in Me and I in you. Run the race I've given you...one with the eternal prize. Live as My Word tells you. As you trust boldly in Me you will see the results around you...sometimes instantly and sometimes in My time. Be patient and wait on Me."

Romans 5:11 - *So now we can rejoice in our wonderful new relationship with God because our Lord Jesus Christ has made us friends of God.*

1 Corinthians 9:24-27 - *Don't you realize that in a race everyone runs, But only one person gets the prize? So run to win! All athletes are disciplined in their training. They do it to win a prize that will fade away, But we do it for an eternal prize. So I run with purpose in every step. I am not just shadowboxing. I discipline my body like an athlete, training it to do what it should. Otherwise, I fear that after preaching to others I myself might be disqualified.*

Hebrews 10:19-24 - *And so, dear brothers and sisters, we can boldly enter heaven's Most Holy Place because of the blood of Jesus. By His death, Jesus opened a new and life-giving way through the curtain into the Most Holy Place. And since we have a great High Priest who rules over God's house, let us go right into the presence of God with sincere hearts fully trusting Him. For our guilty consciences have been sprinkled with Christ's blood to make us clean, our bodies have been washed with pure water. Let us hold tightly without wavering to the hope we affirm, for God* *can be trusted to keep His promise. Let us think of ways to motivate one another to acts of love and good works.*

Hebrews 11:1 *- Faith shows the reality of what we hope for; it is the evidence of things we cannot see.*

Hebrews 11:6 *- And it is impossible to please God without faith Anyone who wants to come to Him must believe that God exists and that He rewards those who sincerely seek Him.*

We say - "I've been married for a long time now, But my spouse doesn't act like he loves or cares about me any more. His friends get more of his attention then I or the kids get. What do I do?"

But God Says - "Stay strong. Be patient. Stay faithful. I will help you through. Don't give up. Keep reflecting Me to your spouse. I will bless you."

1 Corinthians 13:4-7 - *Love is patient and kind. Love is not jealous or boastful or proud or rude. It does not demand its own way. It is not irritable, and it keeps no record of being wronged. It does not rejoice about injustice But rejoices whenever the truth wins out. Love never gives up, never loses faith, is always hopeful, and endures through every circumstance.*

1 Corinthians 16:13-14 - *Be on guard. Stand firm in the faith. Be courageous. Be strong. And do everything with <u>love.</u>*

Hebrews 10:35 - *So do not throw away this confident trust in the Lord. Remember the great reward it brings you!*

Hebrews 13:4a - *Give honor to marriage, and remain faithful to one another in marriage.*

We say - "If you are real, God, how can you let so many people suffer or die?"

But God Says - "I give free will to everyone. Not all choose Me or the path I've planned for them. With wrong choices some bad things can happen. Sometimes it's because of something someone, believer or not, chose to do. One reaps what they sow. Sometimes it affects others as well. Keep your prayers and thoughts and actions focused on what I tell you in My Word. I will not tempt you to make wrong choices. So try not to be a stumbling block to someone else. And when you see someone veering off My path or losing focus off of Me or faith in Me, pray for them. Help them to come back strong. When you ask, I will answer. So sometimes repercussion from wrong choices cause these things. But remember, all will die at one point unless I come back before then. Those who are suffering that you know of, pray for them so I can lessen their suffering. I'm listening. Turn your heart and prayers on Me. Trust Me."

Psalm 37:23 - *The LORD directs the steps of the Godly. He delights in every detail of their lives.*

Proverbs 16:1 - *We can make our own plans, But the LORD gives the right answer.*

Proverbs 16:9 - *We can make our plans, But the LORD determines our steps.*

Galatians 6:5&7 - *For we are each responsible for our own conduct. Don't be misled—you cannot mock the justice of God. You will always harvest what you plant.*

James 1:13&16 - *And remember, when you are being tempted, do not say, "God is tempting me." God is never tempted to do wrong, and He never tempts anyone else. So don't be misled, My dear brothers and sisters.*

We say - "Hey I'm not so bad. Look at our lead choir singer. She talks about the pastor behind his back, flirts with the men of the church. So compared to her I am a saint. So how come I'm not more liked by the people of the church?"

But God Says - "Don't compare yourself to others. Are you sinless? You each will answer for your own sins and wrong choices, unless you seek forgiveness. Believers are under the blood of Jesus Christ, My Son, so you've been forgiven. But when a believer chooses to go against My Word, and your heart does not regret the sin, consequences will come your way. So stay focused on loving Me and doing as I said. Don't judge your neighbor or compare yourself to them. Also don't complain. Walk in love always and you will see love come back to you."

Matthew 7:1-4 - *"Do not judge others, and you will not be judged. For you will be treated as you treat others. The standard you use in judging is the standard by which you will be judged. And why worry about a speck in your friend's eye when you have a log in your own? How can you think of saying to your friend, 'Let me help you get rid of that speck in your eye,' when you can't see past the log in your own eye?"*

Luke 6:37 - *"Do not judge others, and you will not be judged. Do not condemn others, or it will all come back against you. Forgive others, and you will be forgiven...."*

John 8:7 - *They kept demanding an answer, so He stood up again and said, "All right, But let the one who has never sinned throw the first stone!"*

Galatians 6:4 - *Pay careful attention to your own work, for then you will get the satisfaction of a job well done, and you won't need to compare yourself to anyone else.*

We say - "My kids want so much, But we can't afford everything. They always say, 'But so-and-so has those cool shoes. Why can't I have a pair?' We work hard Lord. Why can't we give our kids more?"

But God Says - "Just like when you ask Me for things and I don't always give you exactly what you are asking for or I say no, you sometimes have to do the same for your children. Just because the neighbor has it, doesn't mean it's what is best for your child. I want to give you everything and more as you seek My Kingdom. I want to prosper you so you can bless your children with wonderful things. But as I teach you, even though you can have anything you want — not everything is good for you...you must teach your child the same. I'm not trying to hurt you in any way, But I promise the world will not give your child everything he wants as an adult. Teach him of My love, and let him know if he believes in Me, rests in Me, I will lead him to be prosperous and satisfied in his adult life. You too must learn, it isn't for you to be like your neighbor, have what they have, do what they do. My people are to follow the paths I've planned for them. It is what is best, and My people will have more than enough. You will be blessed to be a blessing. Sometimes your children must wait on some things they want. Other times they have to learn no is the answer. Remember I love you and your children and want what is best for them."

Psalm 37:4 - *Take delight in the LORD, and He will give you your heart's desires.*

Matthew 6:33 - *Seek the Kingdom of God above all else, and live righteously, and He will give you everything you need.*

1 Corinthians 10:23 - *You say, "I am allowed to do anything" — But not everything is good for you. You say, "I am allowed to do anything" — But not everything is beneficial.*

We say - "How come I don't hear You speak to me? I know I'm not the preacher or a missionary, But I'd like to hear from You—Not just read what You told others long ago."

But God Says - "I speak through the Word. I speak through the Holy Spirit living in you. But you have to be listening. You have to remain in Me so I can remain in you. I sometimes speak in dreams. And occasionally through other humans. But know, if someone or some dream tells you something that doesn't line up with My Word, then it wasn't Me talking. So you must stay familiarized with My Word...And ask Me."

Jeremiah 33:3 - *Ask Me and I will tell you remarkable secrets you do not know about things to come.*

Matthew 7:24 - *"Anyone who listens to My teaching and follows it is wise, like a person who builds a house on solid rock...."*

John 10:27-28 - *"...My sheep listen to My voice; I know them, and they follow Me. I give them eternal life, and they will never perish. No one can snatch them away from Me,..."*

Act 2:17 - *'In the last days,' God Says, 'I will pour out My Spirit upon all people. Your sons and daughters will prophesy. Your young men will see visions, and your old men will dream dreams....'*

Hebrews 1:2 - *And now in these final days, He has spoken to us through His Son. God promised everything to the Son as an inheritance, and through the Son He created the universe.*

We say - "I need a miracle. They say You did them back in the day, But I need one now."

But God Says - "I'm the same today as I was yesterday. And I will be the same in the future. I'm always here for you to help you wherever I can, But you have to ask Me and trust that I will provide. Surely, I already know what you need. But I need to know you believe you can receive it from Me...if you'll just ask. In the past, I spoke, I healed, I saved...I still do those things today, But you have to stay close to Me so I can stay close to you. I do the impossible. Those are miracles from Me. Keep your trust in Me, not the world."

Psalm 16:8 - *I know the LORD is always with me. I will not be shaken, for He is right beside me.*

Malachi 3:6a - *"I am the LORD, and I do not change...."*

Matthew 6:33 - *Seek the Kingdom of God above all else, and live righteously, and He will give you everything you need.*

Matthew 19:26 - *Jesus looked at them intently and said, "Humanly speaking, it is impossible. But with God everything is possible."*

John 2:11 - *This miraculous sign at Cana in Galilee was the first time Jesus revealed His glory. And His disciples believed in Him.* (Jesus turned water into wine at a wedding)

Philippians 4:19 - *And this same God who takes care of me will supply all your needs from His glorious riches, which have been given to us in Christ Jesus.*

Hebrews 13:8 - *Jesus Christ is the same yesterday, today, and forever.*

James 4:8 - *Come close to God, and God will come close to you. Wash your hands, you sinners; purify your hearts, for your loyalty is divided between God and the world.*

We say - "Is this what I'm supposed to do? Lord give me a sign. Help me know this is You opening up a new door to me. Is it okay for me to ask?"

But God Says - "It's always okay to ask Me anything. But know I don't always answer the way you want Me to. Sometimes My answer is delayed. Sometimes it's totally different than what you wanted. Sometimes it's exactly what you asked for. And sometimes I even say 'NO.' I see your heart when you ask of Me. If you are just wanting proof I am who I say I am...or to line your own pockets for selfish reasons, then usually I won't answer those. Now, if you are asking to help confirm My will for you, then I will gladly answer. Sometimes in a soft whisper, sometimes in circumstances I allow to come your way. I love you."

Numbers 6:24-26 - *'May the LORD bless you and protect you. May the LORD smile on you and be gracious to you. May the LORD show you His favor and give you His peace.'*

Psalm 5:12 - *For You bless the Godly, O LORD; You surround them with Your shield of love.*

Psalm 84:11 - *For the LORD God is our sun and our shield. He gives us grace and glory. The LORD will withhold no good thing from those who do what is right.*

Matthew 7:7 - *"Keep on asking, and you will receive what you ask for. Keep on seeking, and you will find. Keep on knocking, and the door will be opened to you...."*

John 14:13-14 - *"You can ask for anything in My name, and I will do it, so that the Son can bring glory to the Father. Yes, ask Me for anything in My name, and I will do it."*

Ephesians 1:11 - *Furthermore, because we are united with Christ, we have received an inheritance from God, for He chose us in advance, and He makes everything work out according to His plan.*

We say - "How do I know this is Your will for me? It's gonna cost me more than I have. But inside me, I feel You are leading me this way. Help me know, please? Should I move forward?"

But God Says - "If this is My will for you, I will help you through it. If I ask something of you, I will supply all you need to carry out this plan of mine. Be patient...listen and wait on Me, for My help."

Psalm 27:14 - *Wait patiently for the LORD. Be brave and courageous. Yes, wait patiently for the LORD.*

Psalm 33:20-21 - *We put our hope in the LORD. He is our help and our shield. In Him our hearts rejoice, for we trust in His Holy Name.*

Isaiah 30:18 - *So the LORD must wait for you to come to Him so He can show you His love and compassion. For the LORD is a faithful God. Blessed are those who wait for His help.*

Hebrews 6:15 - *Then Abraham waited patiently, and he received what God had promised.*

Hebrews 10:35-36 - *So do not throw away this confident trust in the Lord. Remember the great reward it brings you! Patient endurance is what you need now, so that you will continue to do God's will. Then you will receive all that He has promised.*

We say - "It's another day of running and rushing from place to place, chore to chore, job to job. My life never slows down. I'm always in a hurry. Not enough time in the day for all I have to do. What am I doing wrong? Plus, I don't feel like I've accomplished anything when all is said and done. Help me, Lord."

But God Says - "Details, details, details. Do you start your day with Me? Is everything on your list important? Does it glorify Me? Does it all grow you closer to Me? Know that I don't call you to do everything. Somethings you may need to let others do. Know what is important in your life."

Psalm 37:5 - *Commit everything you do to the LORD. Trust Him, and He will help you.*

Proverbs 23:4 - *Don't wear yourself out trying to get rich. Be wise enough to know when to quit.*

Matthew 11:28 - *Then Jesus said, "Come to Me, all of you who are weary and carry heavy burdens and I will give you rest...."*

Luke 10:40b-42 - *She came to Jesus and said, "Lord, doesn't it seem unfair to you that my sister just sits here while I do all the work? Tell her to come and help me." But the Lord said to her, "My dear Martha, you are worried and upset over all these details! There is only one thing worth being concerned about. Mary has discovered it, and it will not be taken away from her."*

John 6:63 - *The Spirit alone gives eternal life. Human effort accomplishes nothing. And the very words I have spoken to you are spirit and life.*

Romans 12:2 - *Don't copy the behavior and customs of this world, But let God transform you into a new person by* *changing the way you think. Then you will learn to know God's will for you, which is good and pleasing and perfect.*

We say - "I know what I have done...most of it being things I will never brag about and some being things I won't tell another soul. In fact, I feel guilty. So how can you still love me? I don't deserve your love."

But God Says - "My child, everyone But Jesus has sinned. I love you all in spite of your sins. I loved you so much, My Son paid for all of your sins so you can walk covered in His blood, righteous, living for Me...But only those of you who believe in Me, who let the Holy Spirit live in them, by accepting Jesus as their Savior. I loved you even before you came to Me, and always will."

Isaiah 64:6a - *We are all infected and impure with sin. When we display our righteous deeds, they are nothing But filthy rags.*

Jeremiah 17:9 - *The human heart is the most deceitful of all things, and desperately wicked. Who really knows how bad it is?*

John 3:16 - *"For this is how God loved the world: He gave His one and only Son, so that everyone who believes in Him will not perish But have eternal life...."*

Romans 3:10 - *As the Scriptures say, "No one is righteous—not even one...."*

Romans 3:23 - *For everyone has sinned; we all fall short of God's glorious standard.*

Romans 8:38 - *And I am convinced that nothing can ever separate us from God's love. Neither death nor life, neither angels nor demons, neither our fears for today nor our worries about tomorrow—not even the powers of hell can separate us from God's love.*

1 John 4:8 - *But anyone who does not love does not know God, for God is love.*

1 John 4:16 - *We know how much God loves us, and we have put our trust in His love. God is love, and all who live in love live in God, and God lives in them.*

We say - "Lord, I stopped going to church. I can't be around people right now. But know I'm staying close to You through Your Word and through preaching on television. Is that okay?"

But God Says - "For now it is. I know you are hurting. But know your family is there for you also. Keep your eyes on Me. Stay in the Word, and as soon as you can, return to fellowshipping with your family of believers. Sometimes you are blessed being in the fellowship, and sometimes you are blessing others. So don't stay secluded too long. I love you!"

Psalm 29:2 - *Honor the LORD for the glory of His name. Worship the LORD in the splendor of His holiness.*

Psalm 100:2 - *Worship the LORD with gladness. Come before Him, singing with joy.*

Psalm 122:1,7-9 - *I was glad when they said to me, "Let us go to the house of the LORD." O Jerusalem, may there be peace within your walls and prosperity in your palaces. For the sake of my family and friends, I will say, "May you have peace." For the sake of the house of the LORD our God, I will seek what is best for you, O Jerusalem.*

John 4:23-24 - *"...But the time is coming—indeed it's here now—when true worshipers will worship the Father in spirit and in truth. The Father is looking for those who will worship Him that way. For God is Spirit, so those who worship Him must worship in spirit and in truth."*

Romans 12:1 - *And so, dear brothers and sisters, I plead with you to give your bodies to God because of all He has done for you. Let them be a living and holy* *sacrifice—the kind He will find acceptable. This is truly the way to worship Him.*

Hebrews 13:15 *- Therefore, let us offer through Jesus a continual sacrifice of praise to God, proclaiming our allegiance to His name.*

We say - "Something just isn't right. I don't know what. I trust You, Lord God...Your power, Your promises. But inside I'm not sure You love me enough to come through with what I believe I need. Will You?"

But God Says - "I love you unconditionally, even before you trusted in Me. My love is never-ending. I want to delight you with all your desires when I know your heart is following Me. I filled you with My Holy Spirit. Trust your heart, not your head. What you feel usually comes from thoughts in your mind. Rest in Me and My love, trusting the Holy Spirit in you."

Psalm 20:4 - *May He grant your heart's desires and make all your plans succeed.*

Psalm 37:4 - *Take delight in the LORD, and He will give you your heart's desires.*

Proverbs 10:3 - *The LORD will not let the Godly go hungry, But He refuses to satisfy the craving of the wicked.*

Matthew 6:33 - *"Seek the kingdom of God above all else, and live righteously, and He will give you everything you need."*

John 3:16 - *"For this is how God loved the world: He gave His one and only Son, so that everyone who believes in Him will not perish But have eternal life."*

We say - "The preacher talked about showing compassion in his sermon today. For some reason, it ate at me. I believe I'm compassionate, yet after the message I wasn't so sure. I feel for my fellow man, saved or not, when they go through hard times. I try to pray for them, hoping their situation will turn around...Help however I can. What else can I do? Isn't that being dressed in compassion as You tell us? Feeling and praying for others? And when you see someone asking for a handout, you try to give it?"

But God Says - "I hear you, child of Mine. Your heart is in the right place, But as your preacher was saying there is more to being compassionate than helping those who ask, or praying for those in need. Prayers are great. As My Word tells you, My angels can only work when the door is opened. So again, that is great. Giving is also great, only make sure your heart is willing and joyful as you give. Don't do it begrudgingly...for I know your heart. I believe what your preacher was saying is don't wait for someone to ask you. Be attuned to their needs (friends, family, strangers) and let Me lead you. If you feel the Holy Spirit tugging at your heart, don't turn away. Give compassion to the one in front of you. Sometimes it's only a kind word, or a word of encouragement, But it is something you can give—so give. Just keep your heart open to those around you and let the Holy Spirit lead."

Matthew 25:40 - *"And the King will say, 'I tell you the truth, when you did it to one of the least of these My brothers and sisters, you were doing it to Me!'"*

Romans 12:15 - *Be happy with those who are happy, and weep with those who weep.*

Galatians 6:2 - *Share each other's burdens, and in this way obey the law of Christ.*

Ephesians 4:31-32 - *Get rid of all bitterness, rage, anger, harsh words, and slander, as well as all types of evil* *behavior. Instead, be kind to each other, tenderhearted, forgiving one another, just as God through Christ has forgiven you.*

Philippians 2:4 - Don't look out only for your own interests, But take an interest in others, too.

Colossians 3:12 - Since God chose you to be the holy people He loves, you must clothe yourselves with tenderhearted mercy, kindness, humility, gentleness and patience.

We say - "Did you hear that God? I mean, I'm doing the best that I can and yet I'm the one being criticized. Ooooh. I just want to give them a piece of my mind. Help me. Give me the right words, so maybe next time they'll think twice about putting me down. Grrr."

But God Says - "First, sweet child, calm down. Not every one Says the right thing at the right time. Not even you. If all of my children could pray before opening their mouth, like you just did—talking to Me, telling Me how you felt before jumping on any old response—this world would be a more peaceful place. The good news is one day we, Me and all who believe in Me, Christ Jesus as their Savior, will all be together on the new earth in the new heavens, and My children of God will do that very thing. And in the meantime, remember I have your back. Let Me avenge any one of your enemies and/or your friends in Christ who mess up and say or do the wrong thing against you. After all, you are mere humans living on the first earth I created."

Matthew 5:43-44 - *"You have heard the law that Says, 'Love your neighbor' and hate your enemy. But I say, love your enemies! Pray for those who persecute you!'"*

Luke 6:31 - *"Do to others as you would like them to do to you."*

Romans 12:14 - *Bless those who persecute you. Don't curse them; pray that God will bless them.*

Romans 12:19-21 - *Dear friends, never take revenge. Leave that to the righteous anger of God. For the Scriptures say, "I will take revenge; I will pay them back," Says the LORD. Instead, "If your enemies are hungry, feed them. If they are thirsty, give them something to drink. In doing this, you will heap burning coals of shame on their heads." Don't let evil conquer you, But conquer evil by doing good.*

We say - "My day is not going well. Every thing I've attempted so far today has gone haywire. Is it worth trying to go outside? Everything is so messed up. Why bother?"

But God Says - "You came to Me a few years ago and asked Me into your life. I came. I'm still here. I want your life to be better, But you have to rest totally in Me. Don't keep one foot in the world and the other trusting Me. Trust Me always. Lean on Me. Stay in My Word. My Son died so you could have a good life now, even in abundance, with an amazing eternal life. I want to give you more than you could ever ask for. To enjoy the good life now, you must stay in Me...not the world. And know, when you start to do something to serve Me, Satan will try and stop you or detour you. Your name is written in the Book of Life. He can't remove it, But he can stop you from bringing others to Me."

Matthew 6:24 - *"No one can serve two masters. For you will hate one and love the other; you will be devoted to one and despise the other. You cannot serve God and be enslaved to money."*

John 10:10 - *The thief's purpose is to steal and kill and destroy. My purpose is to give them a rich and satisfying life.*

2 Corinthians 9:8 - *And God will generously provide all you need. Then you will always have everything you need and plenty left over to share with others.*

Ephesians 3:20 - *Now all glory to God, who is able, through His mighty power at work within us, to accomplish infinitely more than we might ask or think.*

Colossians 1:13-14 - *For He has rescued us from the kingdom of darkness and transferred us into the Kingdom of His dear Son, who purchased our freedom and forgave our sins.*

We say - "Is it wrong, Lord, for me to want to make a lot of money using the gift you gave me?"

But God Says - "I've told you many times. I want to bless you in abundance. Everything is mine, and I want to share these good things with My children. I love blessing you, My child, and what I love even more is seeing you use your blessings to bless others. That is My desire. I bless you so you can be a blessing to others. Don't hoard your blessings...share them. When I told you not to love money, I didn't say don't make it. I'm saying again, don't hoard it. Share your blessings with others so I can continue to pour blessings out on you."

Matthew 6:19-21 - *"Don't store up treasures here on earth, where moths eat them and rust destroys them, and where thieves break in and steal. Store your treasures in heaven, where moths and rust cannot destroy, and thieves do not break in and steal."*

Luke 12:15 - *Then He said, "Beware! Guard against every kind of greed. Life is not measured by how much you own."*

1 Timothy 6:6&10 - *Yet true Godliness with contentment is itself great wealth. For the love of money is the root of all kinds of evil. And some people, craving money, have wandered from the true faith and pierced themselves with many sorrows.*

Hebrews 13:5 - *Don't love money; be satisfied with what you have. For God has said, "I will never fail you. I will never abandon you."*

We say - "I don't know what went wrong. In my early years, You led me through so many situations, big and small. Now it seems You don't even hear me anymore. Are You still here with me? Can you hear me call? Nothing in my life seems to be getting better...only worse."

But God Says - "Is your trust still in Me? Are you talking to Me about your trials and tribulations off and on every day? Or are you just calling out in desperation - 'fix this please!'? I know I can fix anything and everything. I am here wanting to help you through. But you know to receive My constant blessings, you must stay with Me. Keep believing My truth. Stand on My Word no matter what others around you are saying and no matter what is happening in your life. Even if people are making fun of your faith in Me. Stand strong. Stay in Me and My Word. I want to help you, keep you in My peace, But you must keep believing and trusting Me."

Zephaniah 3:17 - "...For the LORD your God is living among you. He is a mighty Savior. He will take delight in you with gladness. With His love, He will calm all your fears. He will rejoice over you with joyful songs."

Colossians 1:22-23 - Yet now He has reconciled you to Himself through the death of Christ in His physical body. As a result, He has brought you into His own presence, and you are holy and blameless as you stand before Him without a single fault. But you must continue to believe this truth and stand firmly in it. Don't drift away from the assurance you received when you heard the Good News. The Good News has been preached all over the world, and I, Paul, have been appointed as God's servant to proclaim it.

Hebrews 13:5b - "I will never fail you. I will never abandon you."

We say - "I don't mean to worry about everything. I know You are in control. But You give us free will, and not everyone wants to do what You've called us to do. Some who don't know You are living a life that pleases Satan, causing harm, making so much misery happen around the world. 2020 and 2021 has been the worst years in all my life. I know You have us. But between the news media and the fear around the world, not counting the deaths, it doesn't seem like things are getting better. I try not to worry. And I know You don't make these things happen. But You do allow them. I know, if we keep our faith in You, You will lead us through and we will come out better after we've passed through the horror. But am I strong enough? I worry about all the isolation and how it affects different people different ways. Help us Lord. It's been going on so long. Help us get through it to the other side and keep the people, especially Your people, moving forward. I pray more have turned to You through this...But I hear some people trying to blame You for it. You only do good, and I know this. All won't be good until we are on the new earth in the new heaven. Satan still roams around doing so much damage. Again, help us Lord!"

But God Says - "I am here for you. I am your strength. Don't let go. I will never leave you. Worrying won't add a moment to your life. Stay connected to Me and I will stay connected to you. Worrying does not help. Praise Me through your woes. Stay in faith, knowing I will see you through. One day I will return, and it is getting closer every day. Then all you who have trusted in Me will be immediately risen and transported to the new earth in the new heavens. Oh glorious day!!"

Psalm 28:7 - *The LORD is my strength and shield. I trust Him with all my heart. He helps me, and my heart is filled with joy. I burst out in songs of thanksgiving.*

Luke 12:25-26 - *Can all your worries add a single moment to your life? And if worry can't accomplish a little* *thing like that, what's the use of worrying over bigger things?*

John 15:4 - Remain in Me, and I will remain in you. For a branch cannot produce fruit if it is severed from the vine, and you cannot be fruitful unless you remain in Me.

We say - "I don't mean to think poorly of someone when I see them do or hear them say something. I don't know what they have been through which caused them to act a certain way. I know I make wrong choices sometimes myself...probably a lot of times. I try not to. Please forgive me. And most of all help me not to be so judgmental."

But God Says - "Remember what I told Samuel. I know his heart...and I know your heart. As a child of the Most High God, I see the blood of Jesus covering you. The Holy Spirit lives in you to help you know when you make a misstep saying or doing the wrong thing. Be aware of what He Says to you, because the Holy Spirit, like Jesus, will only tell you what I say. He is there to help you be the best you can be. Stay in My Word, and keep listening for My voice through the Holy Spirit. Listen and obey. I will never leave you stranded, or in a judging mood, as long as you stay with Me."

1 Samuel 16:7 - *But the LORD said to Samuel, "Don't judge by his appearance or height, for I have rejected him. The LORD doesn't see things the way you see them. People judge by outward appearance, But the LORD looks at the heart."*

Psalm 44:21 - *God would surely have known it, for He knows the secrets of every heart.*

John 12:49 - *"I don't speak on My own authority. The Father who sent Me has commanded Me what to say and how to say it."*

Romans 2:1-2 - *You may think you can condemn such people, But you are just as bad, and you have no excuse! When you say they are wicked and should be punished, you are condemning yourself, for you who judge others do these very same things. And we know that God, in His justice, will punish anyone who does such things.*

We say - "I'm so confused. How can we help unbelievers learn about You, if we can't associate with them? Maybe I misunderstood a message that I heard, But I thought You told us to separate ourself from the world."

But God Says - "My sweet child. You are to separate your self from the world by not putting first the earthly things that seem or become so important while living on the earth. Trust Me to provide for you. You need to keep Me first. By keeping Me first, you will watch what you say; how you act; how you react. You will also read My Word and know that what I plan for you is for better tomorrows, prosperous days ahead, and peace. I'm sure what your preacher was saying was don't be best friends with unbelievers. Reach out to them and share the love of God with them. Help them to see God in your actions and reactions. I do, however, tell you not to hangout with people who claim to be believers But keep on willingly and openly sinning. As an individual, separate yourself from bringing sin into your household...stay away from music and shows that don't uplift God, in fact, pretty much do the opposite. Lift Me up in your household, reflecting My love with others. And when you are in the world, walk as Jesus walked—helping the lost; sharing the knowledge of God in your words and actions; helping others to want the peace, joy, and salvation that you have through Jesus Christ the LORD."

Matthew 6:33 - "...*Seek the Kingdom of God above all else, and live righteously, and He will give you everything you need...*"

1 Corinthians 5:10-11 - *But I wasn't talking about unbelievers who indulge in sexual sin, or are greedy, or cheat people, or worship idols. You would have to leave this world to avoid people like that. I meant that you are not to associate with anyone who claims to be a believer yet* *indulges in sexual sin, or is greedy, or worships idols, or is abusive, or is a drunkard, or cheats people. Don't even eat with such people.*

2 Corinthians 6:17 - *"...Therefore, come out from among unbelievers, and separate yourselves from them," Says the LORD. "Don't touch their filthy things, and I will welcome you..."*

We say - "I'm doing the best that I can, But it never seems to be good enough. My boss always wants more, and I already give over 100%. My family wants more of me and less time of me at work. But if I do that, how can we afford to keep having all the nice things we try to provide for our kids. And my wife...I never do enough there. What can I do? How do I please everyone? I'm a good person and try to do what's best for my family, friends, and work. HELP!"

But God Says - "You need only please Me first. When you try to do what I've called you to do, you'll find your wife happier, your kids satisfied (maybe not always happier because they are kids still wanting more), your friends will get on board or maybe they are the wrong friends to have, and at work you will at least find peace because I know you are already giving them more than you should. Take time to read what I tell you, and the rest will fall into place. Keep Me and My Word first. I love you. Always remember that!"

Matthew 6:33 - "...*Seek the Kingdom of God above all else, and live righteously, and He will give you everything you need...*"

Matthew 28:20b - "*And be sure of this: I am with you always, even to the end of the age.*"

Romans 12:2 - *Don't copy the behavior and customs of this world, But let God transform you into a new person by changing the way you think. Then you will learn to know God's will for you, which is good and pleasing and perfect.*

Galatians 1:10 - *Obviously, I'm not trying to win the approval of people, But of God. If pleasing people were my goal, I would not be Christ's servant.*

We say - "My heart is so broken. I don't know if I can go on. The love of my life is gone. Help me to move forward. I don't want to go anywhere or be with anyone. Take me home too. How can I go on?"

But God Says - "It's not your time yet. I still have plans for you to help grow the Kingdom of God. Don't lose heart. You are not alone. My people are watching over you. Keep your faith in Me. Rest in Me."

Psalm 34:18 - *The LORD is close to the brokenhearted; He rescues those whose spirits are crushed.*

1 Timothy 5:3 - *Take care of any widow who has no one else to care for her.*

1 Timothy 5:5 - *Now a true widow, a woman who is truly alone in this world, has placed her hope in God She prays night and day, asking God for His help.*

James 1:27 - *Pure and genuine religion in the sight of God the Father means caring for orphans and widows in their distress and refusing to let the world corrupt you.*

We say - "Are you even real? I grew up in the church. I got saved at 16. I truly thought you were leading me to be a great musician. Now I'm an adult trying to chase that dream I thought you put in my heart, But nothing is working out. Maybe it was all a dream and you were never real. Maybe it was my imagination strong at work."

But God Says - "You know in your heart I am real. Maybe you just got tired of Me leading you. Maybe My plans didn't manifest as fast as you'd hoped. Or just maybe your singing and playing was just a part of Me growing you to the really big plan I have for you. Can you let go, and let Me lead? My big plans are still there for you. Your singing in the church was a stepping stone of you reaching others in My name, bringing them to the Kingdom of God in eternity. I'm still here, waiting for you to let Me lead. Follow Me."

Matthew 10:39 - *If you cling to your life, you will lose it; But if you give up your life for Me, you will find it.*

Galatians 2:20 - *My old self has been crucified with Christ. It is no longer I who live, But Christ lives in me. So I live in this earthly body by trusting in the Son of God, who loved me and gave himself for me.*

Hebrews 12:1-2a - *Therefore, since we are surrounded by such a huge crowd of witnesses to the life of faith, let us strip off every weight that slows us down, especially the sin that so easily trips us up. And let us run with endurance the race God has set before us. We do this by keeping our eyes on Jesus, the champion who initiates and perfects our faith.*

We say - "I thought I was saved. I was doing well. Following what the Word had been telling me. Life was going so well. Then it seemed like I started slipping and things started falling apart. What caused me to fall? I thought I was doing good. But people started asking me things like; why is God letting this virus run rapid around the world? Why is He letting people die? I didn't know the answer, so I started questioning You and questioning my faith. What did I believe in? A God who loves us? Or some image someone else made up?"

But God Says - "I know everyone would love Me to fix everything. Remember, I wanted a perfect world for My creation in the beginning. And it was perfect in the Garden of Eden. But man sinned. I gave Adam and Eve...and every one who walks the earth today...free will. Choices make things happen. I'd love to make everyone pick the right choice each and every time...But then you wouldn't be walking in the freedom I gave. I told you all — choose life or death, good or evil. Know that I love you and will not give up on you. Renew your faith in Me. Stay in the Word. It is true. Trust Me not what man is saying. Know I will see you through. I don't make these bad things happen. Mans free choice brings some of these bad things upon the earth. If you keep your faith in Me, I will see you through...You and everyone who rests in Me."

Joshua 1:9 - *"This is My command—be strong and courageous! Do not be afraid or discouraged. For the LORD your God is with you wherever you go."*

Romans 12:2 - *Don't copy the behavior and customs of this world, But let God transform you into a new person by changing the way you think. Then you will learn to know God's will for you, which is good and pleasing and perfect.*

Hebrews 5:12-14 - *You have been believers so long now that you ought to be teaching others. Instead, you need someone to teach you again the basic things about God's*

Word. You are like babies who need milk and cannot eat solid food. For someone who lives on milk is still an infant and doesn't know how to do what is right. Solid food is for those who are mature, who through training have the skill to recognize the difference between right and wrong.

Hebrews 6:1-12 - So let us stop going over the basic teachings about Christ again and again. Let us go on instead and become mature in our understanding. Surely we don't need to start again with the fundamental importance of repenting from evil deeds and placing our faith in God. You don't need further instruction about baptisms, the laying on of hands, the resurrection of the dead, and eternal judgment. And so, God willing, we will move forward to further understanding. For it is impossible to bring back to repentance those who were once enlightened—those who have experienced the good things of heaven and shared in the Holy Spirit, who have tasted the goodness of the Word of God and the power of the age to come—and who then turn away from God. It is impossible to bring such people back to repentance; by rejecting the Son of God, they themselves are nailing Him to the cross once again and holding Him up to public shame. When the ground soaks up the falling rain and bears a good crop for the farmer, it has God's blessing. But if a field bears thorns and thistles, it is useless. The farmer will soon condemn that field and burn it. Dear friends, even though we are talking this way, we really don't believe it applies to you. We are confident that you are meant for better things, things that come with salvation. For God is not unjust. He will not forget how hard you have worked for Him and how you have shown your love to Him by caring for other believers, as you still do. Our great desire is that you will keep on loving others as long as life lasts, in order to make certain that what you hope for will come true. Then you will not become spiritually dull and indifferent. Instead, you will follow the example of those who are going to inherit God's promises because of their faith and endurance.

We say - "I love You, Lord. I have since I was a young tween. But it's so hard to stay on the straight and narrow. Problems surround me as an adult. I'm struggling. Will I ever get it right?"

But God Says - "Remember, the best fruit ripens slowly. Also remember, growth takes time. You need to nurture your growth through the reading of My Word...through listening to Godly men and women who live for Me and share Me with you...through songs of praise...through fellowshipping with other believers in Me...through worshiping Me. Know that even though you can't see Me working, I am. As long as you keep your faith in Me and My Word in you, I can continue working in you through the Holy Spirit to prune and shape you, as I did Jesus, to be the person I planned for you to be in the beginning. Remember, I knew you before I formed you in your mother's womb. And I had great plans for you then. Still do, and I won't give up...don't you give up either!"

Jeremiah 1:5a - *"I knew you before I formed you in your mother's womb..."*

John 15:2 - *"He cuts off every branch of Mine that doesn't produce fruit, and He prunes the branches that do bear fruit so they will produce even more."*

Galatians 5:22-23 - *But the Holy Spirit produces this kind of fruit in our lives: love, joy, peace, patience, kindness, goodness, faithfulness, gentleness, and self-control. There is no law against these things!*

Hebrews 11:1 - *Faith shows the reality of what we hope for; it is the evidence of things we cannot see.*

We say - "God, I've gone to church almost all of my life...at least as far back as I can remember. One thing that I've never understood is prayer. Sure I close my eyes and bow my head when others pray. I hear friends and family talking about their prayer life and how You answer this one and that one. I also hear how some pray in the morning and afternoon and at night before they go to bed...some for long periods of time. Sad to say, I'm not even sure if you hear my prayers...not that I ask a whole lot. I don't want to bother You. So what do I need to do to get a few of my prayers answered?"

But God Says - "My sweet child. I hear you when you talk to me, not that you do it much. I see you in church being reverent when others are praying, But your thoughts seem to scatter as they pray. So that tells Me your heart isn't in their prayer. I hear you at night when you go to bed, you thank Me for some good things that have happened around you and to you. That makes Me smile because I see you know that good comes from Me. But child, you must always remember to pray from your heart, and believe I want to give you good things, answer sincere prayers. I love you, and what you think and want matter to Me. Believe in Me. Believe in yourself. Believe I can give you all you need and more. Reach out. I'm always listening. And when you pray, know if you'll ask a friend to join you in the prayer, it makes it that much stronger. It shows Me your faith is in Me. I want to bless you with so much...But you must believe to receive."

Jeremiah 29:12 - *In those days when you pray, I will listen.*

Matthew 18:19-20 - *"I also tell you this: If two of you agree here on earth concerning anything you ask, My Father in heaven will do it for you. For where two or three gather together as My followers, I am there among them."*

1 Peter 3:15 - *Instead, you must worship Christ as Lord of your life. And if someone asks about your hope as a believer, always be ready to explain it.*

We say - "Every time I try to change, it never lasts. I want to be all I can for You, for my family, for my friends. Why can't I stick to something. I try to change the way I talk. I try to stop drinking so much. I try to change some of the things I do. I even try to change the way I eat and exercise. But nothing sticks."

But God Says - "I would gladly help you, if you would let Me. But you want to do everything yourself. That's called willpower. Sometimes you have it in boat loads, and other times it's a slow sinking ship. If you'd lean on Me, I could make you stronger. I know the things you are talking about. Like words you say when you think no one is around. Or the occasionally show that you know you really shouldn't be watching. You need to realize, I am with you always. At those times, I am disappointed in you, But I know in your heart you want to please Me. If you would remember, I'm always with you and want to be your strength, you would stick with things through the end letting Me help you. But you have to let go of control, and let Me lead you. So let's start with your thoughts. Working together, we can renew your mind and change your thoughts to be in line with My Word."

Psalm 28:7a - *The LORD is my strength and shield.*

Proverbs 4:23 - *Guard your heart above all else, for it determines the course of your life.*

Romans 12:2 - *Don't copy the behavior and customs of this world, But let God transform you into a new person by changing the way you think. Then you will learn to know God's will for you, which is good and pleasing and perfect.*

We say - "I thought I knew where you wanted me to go, what you wanted me to do. I don't see much difference in my life now from five years ago. What am I doing wrong? How do I move forward in your plans for me."

But God Says - "Have you stayed focused on what I shared with you? Or are you just dabbling in My plans for you, My Word to you? I want to help you in everything. I want you to trust Me in everything. I'm there for you spiritually, emotionally, financially, and physically...But you have to do your part. Trust Me. Believe what I say. Stay in Me. Rest in Me. Keep My Word in you and I will lead you through the Holy Spirit that is within you."

Psalm 32:8 - *The LORD Says, "I will guide you along the best pathway for your life. I will advise you and watch over you."*

Proverbs 3:5-6 - *Trust in the LORD with all your heart; do not depend on your own understanding. Seek His will in all you do, and He will show you which path to take.*

Jeremiah 29:11 - *"For I know the plans I have for you," Says the LORD. "They are plans for good and not for disaster, to give you a future and a hope."*

Matthew 21:22 - *"You can pray for anything, and if you have faith, you will receive it."*

Mark 5:36 - *But Jesus overheard them and said to Jairus, "Don't be afraid. Just have faith."*

John 6:35 - *Jesus replied, "I am the bread of life. Whoever comes to Me will never be hungry again. Whoever believes in Me will never be thirsty."*

Ephesians 2:10 - *For we are God's masterpiece. He has created us anew in Christ Jesus, so we can do the good things He planned for us long ago.*

Philippians 1:6 - *And I am certain that God, who began the good work within you, will continue His work until it is finally finished on the day when Christ Jesus returns.*

We say - "Lord, am I just a face in the crowd to You? Do I even matter to You?"

But God Says - "I had plans for you before I even formed you in your mother's womb. I know you by name; even the hairs on your head — I know how many you have. Of course I care. My child, sometimes I allow things to happen in your life that can be a struggle, But it is meant to strengthen your trust in Me. Don't give up. Persevere through trials that come your way. I have a great plan for you. Follow Me. Let Me lead you."

Jeremiah 1:5 - "I knew you before I formed you in your mother's womb. Before you were born I set you apart and appointed you as My prophet to the nations."

Jeremiah 29:11-13 - "For I know the plans I have for you," Says the LORD. "They are plans for good and not for disaster, to give you a future and a hope. In those days when you pray, I will listen. If you look for Me wholeheartedly, you will find Me."

1 Thessalonians 5:18 - Be thankful in all circumstances, for this is God's will for you who belong to Christ Jesus.

Hebrews 10:35-36 - So do not throw away this confident trust in the Lord. Remember the great reward it brings you! Patient endurance is what you need now, so that you will continue to do God's will. Then you will receive all that He has promised.

We say - "I don't get me, Lord. I know the right thing to do, But sometimes I still don't do it. I mean to...But I make the wrong choices. Why? I really am trying to die to my flesh and live by the Holy Spirit inside of me, But sometimes my flesh is just too strong. Help me!"

But God Says - "I am here for you always. When you find your thoughts straying to something you know you should not even be thinking about or considering, try to put your focus on Me...on My word. I love you child, and I want the best for you. But you have to keep abiding in Me, turning to Me...not away from Me. Grow and rest in My love."

Matthew 28:20b - "...*And be sure of this: I am with you always, even to the end of the age.*"

John 15:5 - "*Yes, I am the vine; you are the branches. Those who remain in Me, and I in them, will produce much fruit. For apart from Me you can do nothing.*"

Romans 12:2 - *Don't copy the behavior and customs of this world, But let God transform you into a new person by changing the way you think. Then you will learn to know God's will for you, which is good and pleasing and perfect.*

Ephesians 3:16-17 - *I pray that from His glorious, unlimited resources He will empower you with inner strength through His Spirit. Then Christ will make His home in your hearts as you trust in Him. Your roots will grow down into God's love and keep you strong.*

We say - "God if You love me, how come all these bad things are happening to me? I had a blowout in the rain on the interstate making me late for work. My husband got laid off. My fence is falling apart and I can't afford to fix it...and another storm is headed our way. My baby is sick and we don't know what is wrong with her. Will she ever get better?"

But God Says - "I love you so much, I sacrificed Jesus, My one and only Son, to save you. Jesus suffered and bled and died for you, for your sins — past, present, and future sins. On the day of judgment you'll see I have forgiven all of your sins. In fact, all your sins were forgiven, paid for by Jesus and forgotten by Me. When you wonder if I love you, look at the cross. Lay your problems at the foot of the cross and let Me lead you through them. Rest in Me. Know that I love you and want to help you through these things. I don't bring any bad on you. Satan loves to test you. I know you will be stronger after each, if you rest on Me, follow My lead. Put all your trust in Me. I will see you through, But you have to follow My lead, rest in Me. You will get through with Me, and you will be better off than before."

Matthew 6:33-34 - *"...Seek the Kingdom of God above all else, and live righteously, and He will give you everything you need...."*

John 3:16-17 - *"For this is how God loved the world: He gave His one and only Son, so that everyone who believes in Him will not perish But have eternal life. God sent His Son into the world not to judge the world, But to save the world through Him."*

John 16:33 - *"I have told you all this so that you may have peace in Me. Here on earth you will have many trials and sorrows. But take heart, because I have overcome the world."*

Romans 5:8 - *But God showed His great love for us by sending Christ to die for us while we were still sinners.*

2 Corinthians 12:9 - *Each time He said, "My grace is all you need. My power works best in weakness." So now I am glad to boast about my weaknesses, so that the power of Christ can work through me.*

James 1:2-4 - *Dear brothers and sisters, when troubles of any kind come your way, consider it an opportunity for great joy. For you know that when your faith is tested, your endurance has a chance to grow. So let it grow, for when your endurance is fully developed, you will be perfect and complete, needing nothing.*

We say - "Lord, I had to sign the divorce papers. What am I going to do? I don't even feel like getting up today. What's the use? A failed marriage...Where do I go from here? How do I go on?"

But God Says - "I am sorry your marriage has come to this. But remember, I have a plan for you...a plan for your future. Keep your trust in Me. Stay close to Me and I will get you through this. I will never leave you, But you must keep Me in your heart through this hardship you are going through. Lean on Me and My Word. Remember, I love you."

Psalm 30:5 - For His anger lasts only a moment, But His favor lasts a lifetime! Weeping may last through the night, But joy comes with the morning.

Isaiah 26:3-4 - You will keep in perfect peace all who trust in you, all whose thoughts are fixed on you! Trust in the LORD always, for the LORD God is the eternal Rock.

Jeremiah 29:11 - "For I know the plans I have for you," Says the LORD. "They are plans for good and not for disaster, to give you a future and a hope...."

Philippians 4:19 - And this same God who takes care of me will supply all your needs from His glorious riches, which have been given to us in Christ Jesus.

Hebrews 4:16 - So let us come boldly to the throne of our gracious God. There we will receive His mercy, and we will find grace to help us when we need it most.

Hebrews 13:5-6 - Don't love money; be satisfied with what you have. For God has said, "I will never fail you. I will never abandon you." So we can say with confidence, "The LORD is my helper, so I will have no fear. What can mere people do to me?"

We say - "I've always wanted a house on the beach. My friend has one. Why can't I?"

But God Says - "First let Me say, you have the power to make that happen when you can. I'm not stopping you. Yes, I am all powerful, But I delegated authority to mankind in the Garden of Eden, giving man dominion over your choices. Even after Adam and then mankind failed, I sent My Son to take back Satan's authority. Now Jesus gives authority back to those of you who come under the covenant of His blood, by believing in Him as your Savior. Again, you are still free to choose. Make wise choices. Notice, by all of mankind's choices, the world is in the shape it is in now...and you by your choices. You are living the life you've chosen for yourself. Invite Me in to help you in your sicknesses—finances—relationships and more; direct you on the path I've planned for you, comfort you through sorrows and loss...I will gladly help you as a believer. But you must put Me first. My Word. I love you and want the best for you...even a home on a beach, if that is what is best for you. But don't want it because your friend has it. Want what is best for you; to be all you can be as you grow the Kingdom of God for mankind for eternity. Walk in My love for others."

Genesis 1:27-28a - *So God created human beings in His own image. In the image of God He created them; male and female He created them. Then God blessed them and said "Be fruitful and multiply. Fill the earth and govern it. Reign over..."*

Exodus 20:17 - *"You must not covet your neighbor's house. You must not covet your neighbor's wife, male or female servant, ox or donkey, or anything else that belongs to your neighbor."*

Ecclesiastes 6:9 - Enjoy what you have rather than desiring what you don't have. Just dreaming about nice things is meaningless—like chasing the wind.

John 15:12 - "...This is My commandment: Love each other in the same way I have loved you...."

Philippians 2:3 - Don't be selfish; don't try to impress others. Be humble, thinking of others as better than yourselves.

We say - "What is wrong with me? I gave my heart to Christ a few months ago, But I find I still enjoy doing things I'm pretty sure God doesn't like. How do I stop myself from sinning? How do I walk in His righteousness?"

But God Says - "Before I sent my Son to save you, it was a struggle. Man could not keep the law perfectly. Only Jesus did, and then He gave His life for you and paid the price for all your sins...old and new. You need to stay in My word and know you are under His blood, making you the righteousness of God through Christ. His blood and your faith makes you perfect in My sight. Grow your faith by trusting in Me and leaning on Me to live a happy abundant life. Let your joy come from Me and your relationship with Me will grow. I love you and always will. Stay in My Word and it will help guide you and help you make more informed decisions as I've given you free choices."

Daniel 9:21 - *As I was praying, Gabriel, whom I had seen in the earlier vision, came swiftly to me at the time of the evening sacrifice.*

Romans 5:17 - *For the sin of this one man, Adam, caused death to rule over many. But even greater is Gods wonderful grace and His gift of righteousness, for all who receive it will live in triumph over sin and death through this one man, Jesus Christ.*

Romans 5:21 - *So just as sin ruled over all people and brought them to death, now God's wonderful grace rules instead, giving us right standing with God and resulting in eternal life through Jesus Christ out Lord.*

2 Corinthians 5:21 - *For God made Christ, who never sinned, to be the offering for our sin, so that we could be made right with God through Christ.*

Hebrews 9:12 - *With His own blood—not the blood of goats and calves—He entered the Most Holy Place once for all time and secured our redemption forever.*

We say - "I am so far from perfect. What can I do to get better?"

But God Says - "You are made perfect through My Son, Jesus Christ. I made you perfect when you heard the good news and received Jesus as your Savior. In your flesh, you will always make missteps and mistakes, But your faith in Jesus makes you pure. Your belief in Him covers you in His blood, making you perfect—and that is what I see. Stay in My Word and it will help you live a more fruitful and blessed life every day reflecting Me."

Hebrews 10:14 -17 - *For by that one offering He forever made perfect those who are being made holy. And the Holy Spirit also testifies that this is so. For He Says, "This is the new covenant I will make with My people on that day, Says the LORD: I will put My laws in their hearts, and I will write them on their minds." Then He Says, "I will never again remember their sins and lawless deeds."*

2 Corinthians 3:16-18 - *But whenever someone turns to the Lord, the veil is taken away. For the Lord is the Spirit, and wherever the Spirit of the Lord is, there is freedom. So all of us who have had that veil removed can see and reflect the glory of the Lord. And the Lord—who is the Spirit—makes us more and more like Him as we are changed into His glorious image.*

We say - "Life is always a struggle. I go through the same thing week after week. Will it ever get better?"

But God Says - "I want to help you grow in life and grow in your faith in Me. I give you free will. Notice the choices you are making in the decisions of your life. Are you following My lead? If you would get into the Word and really listen to what I say, you will make smarter choices for your eternal life and thus make your earthly life a better place for you. I have favors I'd love to bestow upon you, But you must keep your heart and mind on Me and My ways. Your tomorrow will be so much better. Walk in My love. Be gentle with others. Humble yourself. Take the little you have and bless others with it. You'll be amazed at how your life will start turning when you put others before yourself."

Job 8:5-7 - But if you pray to God and seek the favor of the Almighty. And if you are pure and live with integrity, He will surely rise up and restore your happy home. And though you started with little, you will end with much.

Ephesians 4:2-4 - Alway be humble and gentle. Be patient with each other, making allowance for each other's faults because of your love. Make every effort to keep yourselves united in the Spirit, binding yourselves together with peace. For there is one body and one Spirit, just as you have been called to one glorious hope for the future.

We say - "The world is falling apart. A virus has been inflicted on the world, and we are now shut down all around. To listen to the news and the politicians it's going to destroy us all, and they don't hesitate to point fingers. The sad thing is, man created this virus and now mankind is having to go through it all. Laws for our safety have been poured down on us. I try to follow them, But mostly I know You've got me. Psalm 91 gives me the security I need to travel through this insanity that has been poured out on the world. So many have suffered, some even died from this horrific terror that was created. Even some of us who believe in You have been taken from this world. I know Your desire is for all of us to be healed, whole, and living a sharing caring life for our fellow man, sharing Your Word, Your Good News, so that when the end comes we who believe will be transported to the new earth in the new heavens that You will create. But in the meantime we have to live through the choices of mankind. Help me follow Your will for me through it all. Help me keep my eyes on You and Your Word and stay at peace. I love You Lord, and I thank You for all your blessings and love that you continue to favor us with. Help me to stay strong for others."

But God Says - "My sweet child. You are in the world But not of the world. Keep your faith in Me. I will be your strength through it all. My Word is a promise to you and to all who believe in Me. But you and they must keep your trust, your faith, in Me. Don't doubt. I will protect you. I am your shield. And remember, when things get tough, if you'll rest in Me, I will carry you through."

Psalm 18:1-2 - *I love You, LORD; You are my strength. The LORD is my rock, my fortress, and my savior; my God is my rock, in whom I find protection. He is my shield, the power that saves me, and my place of safety.*

Psalm 68:19 - *Praise the LORD; praise God our Savior! For each day He carries us in His arms.*

We say - "I know You called us to go downtown and feed the hungry, But LORD do You know what has been happening down there lately? Of course, You do. You know everything. But from the news reports a lot of people have been hurt on the streets. We could be hurt. How can You ask us to go there, knowing the trouble that is going on in this world?"

But God Says - "Haven't I always told you to not be afraid...I'll be with you...I won't be turning my back on you. I picked you! So don't tell Me you can't do something I've called you to do. No matter your age, your wisdom, your abilities, haven't I told you that anything you lack I will provide. And remember—I will take care of you, protect you! Trust me!"

Deuteronomy 31:6 - "So be strong and courageous! Do not be afraid and do not panic before them. For the LORD your God will personally go ahead of you. He will neither fail you nor abandon you."

Jeremiah 1:7-8 - *The LORD replied, "Don't say, 'I'm too young,' for you must go wherever I send you and say whatever I tell you. And don't be afraid of the people, for I will be with you and will protect you. I, the LORD, have spoken!"*

John 15:16 - *You didn't choose Me. I chose you. I appointed you to go and produce lasting fruit, so that the Father will give you whatever you ask for, using My name.*

1 Peter 2:9 - *But you are not like that, for you are a chosen people. You are royal priests, a holy nation, God' very own possession. As a result, you can show others the goodness of God, for He called you out of the darkness into His wonderful light.*

We say - "I don't understand. I love You Lord. I don't fear You. You are my everything. So why does the Word tell me to fear You in some of the verses I've read. I'm still new to understanding some of the things You tell us. Help me."

But God Says - "It's okay. As you keep My Word you will understand more and more. The fear I speak of is the fear of what I can do and will do to those who don't invite Me into their hearts. Those who choose not to believe in Jesus and His death and resurrection will be sent to hell for eternity. That is the fear I am talking about. Those of you who chose to come to Me and are under the blood of Jesus I will protect and bless. And as you grow in Me and My Word your joy will lead your family to want to know Me as well. In the meantime, through your prayers and requests for their protection, I will keep reaching out to them. So keep loving Me and reading My Word. God bess you, child of mine."

Psalm 112:1-9 - *Praise the LORD! How joyful are those who fear the LORD and delight in obeying His commands. Their children will be successful everywhere; an entire generation of Godly people will be blessed. They themselves will be wealthy, and their good deed will last forever. Light shines in the darkness for the Godly. They are generous, compassionate, and righteous. Good comes to those who lend money generously and conduct their business fairly. Such people will not be overcome by evil. Those who are righteous will be long remembered. They do not fear bad news; they confidently trust the LORD to care for them. They are confident and fearless and can face their foes triumphantly. They share freely and give generously to those in need. Their good deeds will be remembered forever. They will have influence and honor.*

We say - "The world is crazy. So much is happening all around me. Help me, Lord!"

But God Says - "Keep your eyes on Me. Keep thanking Me, acknowledging your faith and love in Me, and I will keep you free and safe in Me. Rest in Me, and I will protect you. I want to carry you through anything and all things that come your way. I made this day and have great plans for you. Stay in faith in Me and My Word."

Psalm 118:1 - *Give thanks to the LORD, for He is good! His faithful love endures forever.*

Psalm 118:5-6 - *In my distress I prayed to the LORD, and the LORD answered me and set me free. The LORD is for me, so I will have no fear. What can mere people do to me?*

Psalm 118:8 - *It is better to take refuge in the LORD than to trust in people.*

Psalm 118:14 - *The LORD is my strength and my song; He has given me victory.*

Psalm 118:24 - *This is the day the LORD has made. We will rejoice and be glad in it.*

We say - "I've grown up in the church. I tried to be good. I tried following all the rules of the church and of the Bible, But it's just too hard. As a kid, I followed my parents' lead. But as an adult, I just don't get all the rules and regulations. Times are different now. How can rules still be the same?"

But God Says - "It sounds like you followed Me with your head, not your heart. I want your heart to come to Me. Give your heart to Me, and I will help you through. The only rule or law, as you say, I give is for you to love Me above everyone and everything else, and for you to love your neighbor as you love yourself. Put Me first. Then I can pour out My blessings and favor on you as I really want to do. Once you've come to Me with your whole heart you will know and feel the difference. I keep My promises. I will help you, lift you up in your times of need—But you must continue to rest in Me, trusting Me with your heart. I love you. Keep seeking Me and you will find Me. I'm right here waiting."

Psalm 145:1-21 - *I will exalt You, my God and King, and praise Your name forever and ever. I will praise You every day; yes, I will praise You forever. Great is the LORD! He is most worthy of praise! No one can measure His greatness. Let each generation tell its children of your mighty acts; let them proclaim your power. I will meditate on your majestic, glorious splendor and your wonderful miracles. Your awe-inspiring deeds will be on every tongue; I will proclaim your greatness. Everyone will share the story of your wonderful goodness; they will sing with joy about your righteousness. The LORD is merciful and compassionate, slow to get angry and filled with unfailing love. The LORD is good to everyone. He showers compassion on all His creation. All of Your works will thank*

You, LORD, and Your faithful followers will praise You. They will speak of the glory of Your kingdom; they will give examples of Your power. They will tell about Your mighty deeds and about the majesty and glory of Your reign. For Your kingdom is an everlasting kingdom. You rule throughout all generations. The LORD always keeps His promises; He is gracious in all He does. The LORD helps the fallen and lifts those bent beneath their loads. The eyes of all look to You in hope; You give them their food as they need it. When You open Your hand, You satisfy the hunger and thirst of every living thing. The LORD is righteous in everything He does; He is filled with kindness. The LORD is close to all who call on Him, yes, to all who call on Him in truth. He grants the desire of those who fear Him; He hears their cries for help and rescues them. The LORD protects all those who love Him, But He destroys the wicked. I will praise the LORD, and may everyone on earth bless His holy name forever and ever.

We say - "I've been a believer since I was a teenager. Every time the doors of the church were opened, I was on the inside. I love You, Lord and try to do all You tell me to do. But when it comes to the money thing, Lord, the world is different now. It takes every penny I make to keep food in our stomachs and a roof over our heads. I don't have any left over—ever. So how can You expect me to give You ten percent of my earnings before I care for my family? I'm the head of the house, the provider, the caretaker. Even schools these days are expensive, and that's with my kids in public school. There is no money left over. I am so sorry. Please understand and forgive me."

But God Says - "Jesus paid the price once and for all for all of your sins' past, present, and future. So your Salvation is safe in His blood. Don't you worry about that. And son, I see you struggling every day to make ends meet. Know that I am here to provide; I am here to care for you and your family. My Word tells you to give Me, your church, ten percent off the top. If you trust in Me and in My Words, you will do this. I even tell you to test me in this. It doesn't make sense in the natural to you, But know by the supernatural — Me — the ninety percent you leave for yourself I will stretch further. And as you keep trusting Me, your income will grow to overflow. You just have to trust Me and My Word first. I love you, son. Trust Me."

Proverbs 3:9-10 - *Honor the LORD with your wealth and with the best part of everything you produce. Then He will fill your barns with grain, and your vats will overflow with good wine.*

Malachi 3:10 - *"Bring all the tithes into the storehouse so there will be enough food in My Temple. If you do," Says the LORD of Heaven's Armies, "I will open the windows of heaven for you. I will pour out a blessing so great you won't have enough room to take it in! Try it! Put Me to the test!"*

Matthew 6:33 - *"...Seek the Kingdom of God above all else, and live righteously, and He will give you everything you need...."*

We say - "Is it wrong to want more?"

But God Says - "Through Me you can have everything you need and more. I will supply it."

Matthew 6:33-34 - *Seek the Kingdom of God above all else, and live righteously, and He will give you everything you need. "So don't worry about tomorrow, for tomorrow will bring its own worries. Today's trouble is enough for today."*

John 10:10 - *"...I have come that they may have life, and that they may have it more abundantly."*

Philippians 4:19 - *And this same God who takes care of me will supply all your needs from His glorious riches, which have been given to us in Christ Jesus.*

We say - "I am so afraid. I can't go or do anything. I can't even be around people. I stay home and stay inside living in fear. Help me, Lord!"

But God Says - "I want to help you. Know that fear is not from Me. Know that spirit of fear that surrounds you is from Satan himself. He wants to keep you bound up tight. He knows you are saved, because you came to Me as a small boy and asked Me into your heart. I have never left you. It's you who have chosen to turn away from Me. I protect you as much as you allow Me to, But the fear that you dwell in keeps Me locked out. You're focused on your situations instead of Me. You have to turn to Me. Trust in Me. Rest in Me. Love Me. And you MUST love yourself. You had a very bad experience as a young adult and your best friend let you down. That built a wall of anger, then hate and pity. Along with it grew sadness. So let's back up and start there. Pray for your ex-friend. Pray, forgiving the wrong that he did to you, and ask Me to bless him. That right there will start melting your heart allowing anger to be purged from within, thus helping you to start blocking Satan from roaring in your head about things to be afraid of. I truly want to help you, But you must clear the path between you and Me. Forgive those who hurt you so I can forgive you and love on you and bless you and protect you. Focus on Me, not your fears. And take it one day at a time...one minute at a time. Stay in the moment. Don't look back or try to figure out your future. Look at Me. Let Me guard you from the evil one. As you do, you will see the fear melting off of you. You will find strength to step back out into the world and be among other righteous people (fellow believers)...just keep your heart focused on Me. I will be your strength. And I will fill you with peace instead of fear. The truth be known, Satan fears you. He knows all I've done for you in your past and if you start remembering the miracles and the blessings that came your way, and then start sharing them with others, think of all the people you

might bring to salvation in Jesus Christ. Let Me help you. Walk in love, My love."

Deuteronomy 31:6 - *"...So be strong and courageous! Do not be afraid and do not panic before them. For the LORD your God will personally go ahead of you. He will neither fail you nor abandon you."*

Joshua 1:9 - *He commands us to be strong and courageous. Not afraid or discouraged. The LORD our God is with us everywhere we go!!!*

Psalm 28:7 - *The LORD is my strength and shield. I trust Him with all my heart. He helps me, and my heart is filled with joy. I burst out in songs of thanksgiving.*

Psalm 29:11 - *The LORD gives His people strength. The LORD blesses them with peace.*

John 16:33 - *"I have told you all this so that you may have peace in Me. Here on earth you will have many trials and sorrows. But take heart, because I have overcome the world."*

1 Corinthians 16:13-14 - *Be on guard. Stand firm in the faith. Be courageous. Be strong. And do everything with love.*

Philippians 4:13 - *For I can do everything through Christ, who gives me strength.*

2 Thessalonians 3:2 - *Pray, too, that we will be rescued from wicked and evil people, for not everyone is a believer. But the Lord is faithful; He will strengthen you and guard you from the evil one.*

2 Timothy 1:7 - *For God has not given us a spirit of fear and timidity, But of power, love, and self-discipline.*

We say - "I'm just a nobody...or should I say a somebody. But I can't make a difference in this world. Things are falling apart all around me. It's too late."

But God Says - "It's not too late. You are a part of the body of Me. As you walk the earth, when you are remembering Me and keeping Me first in your life, your actions, thoughts, and words should reflect Me. As long as you keep depending on Me and you stay in My Word, trusting Me, trusting the Word, you will reflect Me and help our family, the family of God, grow as I have called you to do from the beginning, bringing more to Salvation. I picked you before you were born. Trust Me. I know you and you are mine, sweet child, and I have plans to use you to help grow the Kingdom of God."

Proverbs 16:3 - *Commit your actions to the LORD, and your plans will succeed.*

Mark 16:15-16 - *And then He told them, "Go into all the world and preach the Good News to everyone. Anyone who believes and is baptized will be saved. But anyone who refuses to believe will be condemned."*

John 3:16 - *"For this is how God loved the world; He gave His One and only Son, so that everyone who believes in Him will not perish But have eternal life."*

1 Corinthians 12:27 - *If one part suffers, all the parts suffer with it, and if one part is honored, all the parts are glad.*

Ephesians 5:29-30 - *No one hates his own body But feeds and cares for it, just as Christ cares for the church. And we are members of His body.*

We say - "I gave my life to You when I asked you into my heart. But I still mess up. Some people try to tell me it wasn't real, But I know my decision to follow you was real, is real. I love you. Just sometimes my flesh wins out. Yes, I'm the one who let it win, But I don't mean to. And then these thoughts come in my head saying maybe others know better than me. Maybe it wasn't real—my Salvation that is. But in my heart I know it was. Help me Lord!"

But God Says - "Some people hear the Good News and get excited, But as soon as they are out from around the group at church or those who were encouraging them, they forget all they heard. It wasn't taken into their hearts and etched there. And sometimes people hear the message and accept Me as their Savior, But then when the trials of the world get rough, they start to doubt their connection to Me. Remember, I tell you in My Word trials will come. But, if you stick with Me, I will get you through. When you come to Me sincerely with your whole heart, you are saved. Just because some believers let their flesh take over after a time of trial, it doesn't mean I'm letting go of them...it's them letting go of Me. Think of the time Peter asked if he could step out on the water and walk to Me. I said come. As he started walking on water he was fine, till he took his eyes off of Me and put them on the storm around Him. I was still there. And when he cried out as he was going under, I pulled him up. Remember, I'm always there for those who have come to Me. Then there are others who heard My Good News of Salvation, took it to heart, etched it deep, and kept reading My Word and hearing more messages, growing their faith deeper and deeper. The only ones not saved, are those who refused Me or listened, understood, and still stepped away. They will suffer in eternity. But you child, are saved. Your name was written in the Book of Life never to be erased. I love you. And I know you love Me. Share Me boldly with others around you and grow the Kingdom of God."

Matthew 13:5-6 - Other seeds fell on shallow soil with underlying rock. The seeds sprouted quickly because the soil was shallow. But the plants soon wilted under the hot sun, and since they didn't have deep roots, they died.

Matthew 21:21-22 - Then Jesus told them, "I tell you the truth, if you have faith and don't doubt, you can do things like this and much more. You can even say to this mountain, 'May you be lifted up and thrown into the sea,' and it will happen. You can pray for anything, and if you have faith, you will receive it."

Mark 11:24-25 - I tell you, you can pray for anything, and if you believe that you've received it, it will be yours. But when you are praying, first forgive anyone you are holding a grudge against, so that your Father in heaven will forgive your sins, too."

We say - "The church is talking about going on a mission trip. Lord, I want to go and be a part of it, But I don't know if I can be of any help. What can I do?"

But God Says - "If you feel Me calling you to go, then go. But don't go because everyone else is going. Follow My lead. Remember, when I call you to go or do something to grow the Kingdom of God, I will supply all you need. My plan is to share My Word with others through My believers to grow My Kingdom for eternity. You are My sheep, hear My call and follow Me."

Mark 16:15 - *And then He told them, "Go into all the world and preach the Good News to everyone."*

Luke 11:28 - *Jesus replied, "But even more blessed are all who hear the word of God and put it into practice."*

Luke 12:31 - *Seek the Kingdom of God above all else, and He will give you everything you need.*

We say - "I am blessed by You to be retired and still living an active life. Sad to say, one thing I felt led by You to do has now gone on for almost four years. I don't think I'm still helping. If it's time for me to step away, let me know. I don't want to harm anyone or anything. I only want to be a help. Lead me Lord!"

But God Says - "You heard Me call you into that position in your life. Keep looking to Me for your guidance and direction. I will let you know when it's time to move on. Keep Me first, keep loving Me, and keep letting Me lead you. I will continue to bless you as you bless others with your time and commitment. Keep them in your prayers as well, lifting them up to Me. I will reach out to them even more."

John 1:16 - From His abundance we have all received one gracious blessing after another.

John 14:15-17 - "If you love Me, obey My commandments. And I will ask the Father, and He will give you another Advocate, who will never leave you. He is the Holy Spirit, who leads into all truth. The world cannot receive Him, because it isn't looking for Him and doesn't recognize Him. But you know Him, because He lives with you now and later will be in you...."

John 14:21 - "Those who accept My commandments and obey them are the ones who love Me. And because they love Me, My Father will love them. And I will love them and reveal Myself to each of them."

We say - "This world is not getting back to living as fast as I thought it would. I know what my prayers to You were...to kill off the virus that has swept through the world and show Your glory through it all."

But God Says - "Child, remember, I see the big picture, and My timing is always right. Wait on Me. Never waiver in your faith in Me. Sin is in the world and bad things happen, But I do answer prayers of My people...But in My time and My way. Stay in rest and trust Me."

Isaiah 55:8 - "My thoughts are nothing like your thoughts" Says the LORD. "And My ways are far beyond anything you could imagine."

John 15:7 - But if you remain in Me and My Words remain in you, you may ask for anything you want, and it will be granted!

John 17:22-23 - I have given them the glory You gave Me so they may be one as We are One. I am in them and You are in Me. May they experience such perfect unity that the world will know that You sent Me and that You love them as much as You love Me.

Romans 4:20-21 - Abraham never wavered in believing God's promise. In fact, his faith grew stronger, and in this he brought glory to God. He was fully convinced that God is able to do whatever He promises.

Romans 5:15 - But there is a great difference between Adam's sin and God's gracious gift. For the sin of this one man, Adam, brought death to many. But even greater is God's wonderful grace and His gift of forgiveness to many through this other man, Jesus Christ.

Ephesians 2:10 - *For we are God's masterpiece. He has created us anew in Christ Jesus, so we can do the good things He planned for us long ago.*

Ephesians 4:26b-27 - *Don't let the sun go down while you are still angry for anger gives a foothold to the devil.*

We say - "You tell me to write, But sometimes it's weeks and months between my writing. In the beginning, You gave me one story after another...But now that I'm writing non-fiction, it moves so much slower. Help me. I hope one day we go back to my stories being fiction while sharing the real true You...the One who loves us and never leaves us. But then I remember, not my will But Thine. Keep me focused. Keep me moving forward—please!!!"

But God Says - "Like Paul, you will be proud to know that you did not run the race in vain, even though at times it doesn't look to you like you are moving forward. Know that the work you do for Me, sharing Me with others is not useless. I called you for a reason; To share My love with others, letting them know I will not ever leave them when they come to Me and choose to ask Me into their hearts. Thank you, for sharing Me."

Philippians 2:12-16 - *Dear friends, you always followed my instructions when I was with you. And now that I am away it is even more important. Work hard to show the results of your salvation, obeying God with deep reverence and fear. For God is working in you, giving you the desire and the power to do what pleases Him. Do everything without complaining and arguing, so that no one can criticize you. Live clean, innocent lives as children of God, shining like bright lights in a world full of crooked and perverse people. Hold firmly to the Word of life; then on* *the day of Christ's return, I will be proud that I did not run the race in vain and that my work was not useless.*

the day of Christ's return, I will be proud that I did not run the race in vain and that my work was not useless.

We say - "You'd think I'd be at peace. For some reason, all I hear from others is negative and sad things. I find myself listening and feeling down. I used to be so positive and happy. What is going on with me?"

But God Says - "You said it. You are listening to others. You need to be listening to Me. Know that I am the truth. They tell you what they hear or see, But I've already told you how to stay in My peace and in My rest. Focus on Me. Focus on what is good and lovely. Stay in faith, trusting Me. I give you power and strength, Mine, when you lean on Me."

Philippians 4:4-9 - *Always be full of joy in the Lord. I say it again—rejoice! Let everyone see that you are considerate in all you do. Remember, the Lord is coming soon. Don't worry about anything; instead, pray about everything. Tell God what you need, and thank Him for all He has done. Then you will experience God's peace, which exceeds anything we can understand. His peace will guard your hearts and minds as you live in Christ Jesus. And now dear brothers and sisters, one final thing. Fix your thoughts on what is true, and honorable, and right and pure and lovely, and admirable. Think about things that are excellent and worthy of praise. Keep putting into practice all you learned and received from Me—everything you heard from Me and saw Me doing. Then the God of peace will be with you.*

1 Timothy 6:12 - *Fight the good fight for the true faith. Hold tightly to the eternal life to which God has called you, which you have declared so well before many witnesses.*

2nd Timothy 1:7 - *For God has not given us a spirit of fear and timidity, But of power, love, and self-discipline.*

Hebrews 3:6 - *But Christ, as the Son, is in charge of God's entire house. And we are God's house, if we keep our courage and remain confident in our hope in Christ.*

We say - "Lord, help me. When I go to a funeral lately, some of these preachers get into the ten commandments. I know, before Christ, following the ten commandments and the priest making blood sacrifices over and over for Your people was the only way to be forgiven of their sins. Praise God for the new covenant we are under — the Blood of Jesus! You made the way because you knew we were all sinners and we could not walk sinless. Jesus did that for us and then paid with His blood. If we believe and receive Him as our Savior, we are under the new covenant. Please help these pastors be more aware of how they are sharing You God. You are love. You are full of forgiveness. We just need to follow You, rest in You, trust You."

But God Says - "Remember, I gave free choice to everyone. I do pray all My people share My love and forgiveness with others and what Jesus did for them. The only one you can control is yourself, child. So stay in faith and love in Me and keep sharing Me with everyone. Even pastors who are trying to bring the lost to Me. Pray as you listen, pray for the pastor, pray for the nonbelievers, to hear the true message of My love and forgiveness."

Hebrews 8:10-13 - *But this is the new covenant I will make with the people of Israel on that day, Says the LORD: I will put My laws in their minds, and I will write them on their hearts. I will be their God, and they will be My people. And they will not need to teach their neighbors, nor will they need to teach their relatives, saying, 'You should know the LORD.' For everyone, from the least to the greatest will know Me already. And I will forgive their wickedness and I will never again remember their sins." When God speaks of a "new" covenant, it means He has made the first one obsolete. It is now out of date and will soon disappear.*

We say - "God, am I doing all I can? Do people see You when they look at me? I want to reflect You in all I say and do. Help me Lord!"

But God Says - "As you keep in My Word, growing in knowledge of My Word, you will reflect Me more and more. Your thoughts or ways will never be exactly as Mine are, But as long as you keep searching for Me and My ways, and leaning on Me, you will light up from within reflecting My glory in you. I will fill your temple with My glory and others will see you in Me. So keep on asking and receiving what you asked Me for, believing and walking in faith, and others will see Me in you. Keep your heart filled with My Words and you will overflow with treasury from Me."

Isaiah 55:8-9 - *"My thoughts are nothing like your thoughts," Says the LORD. "And My ways are far beyond anything you could imagine. For just as the heavens are higher than the earth, so My ways are higher than your ways and My thoughts higher than your thoughts...."*

Haggai 2:7b-9 - "I will fill this place with glory, Says the LORD of Heaven's Armies. The silver is mine, and the gold is mine, Says the LORD of Heaven's Armies. The future glory of this Temple will be greater than its past glory, Says the LORD of Heaven's Armies. And in this place I will bring peace. I, the LORD of Heaven's Armies, have spoken!"

Matthew 7:7 - "Keep on asking, and you will receive what you ask for. Keep on seeking, and you will find. Keep on knocking, and the door will be opened to you...."

Matthew 12:35-37 - *"...A good person produces good things from the treasury of a good heart, and an evil person produces evil things from the treasury of an evil heart. And*

I tell you this, you must give an account on judgment day for every idle word you speak. The words you say will either acquit you or condemn you."

We say - "I want to ask You to help me. Give me more Word knowledge, and more power in what I share with others trying to help them walk in faith not fear. Help me understand what You tell me on how to relate Your Word to them. I want to come boldly to You when I ask for wisdom or help, I do. But then I hear people put me down for believing that I am one of Your people who You love dearly. I know that You mean every Word to me, and to others you have me share You with. By Your Word — I am healed. I am whole. I am safe. I am protected. But I'm just a woman, widow, mother, and grandmother. No one special by what others say—But LORD, You make me special. I believe what You tell me, But not everyone wants to hear my conviction. I'm so sorry if I'm letting you down. Help me be bolder!"

But God Says - "You, child, cannot make people take to heart and walk in faith in what My Word Says to you and should say to them. But you can keep sharing, knowing My Word is truth and it is for all who take it to heart and walk in faith. It's their choice, dear one. You just keep coming to Me, asking for more wisdom. I will give it to you generously as I've done in the past. Don't give up. You are doing what I called you to do. You are not responsible for how they respond to the seeds you plant. Just keep loving and trusting Me for all your needs and direction. And keep sharing Me in your love for Me. It is up to them if they listen or not. I promise, I will not let you down."

James 1:5-8 - If you need wisdom, ask our generous God, and He will give it to you. He will not rebuke you for asking. But when you ask Him, be sure that your faith is in God alone. Do not waver, for a person with divided loyalty is as unsettled as a wave of the sea that is blown and tossed by the wind. Such people would not expect to receive anything from the Lord. Their loyalty is divided between

God and the world, and they are unstable in everything they do.

1 John 3:21-22 - Dear friends, if we don't feel guilty, we can come to God with bold confidence. And we will receive from Him whatever we ask because we obey Him and do the things that please Him.

We say - "Are you real? I have friends who believe in You. I want to. But how can I be sure?"

But God Says - "I am real...But you have to believe in Me by faith. Even some of My followers didn't believe I died and was resurrected by God until they saw Me and My scars. Read about Thomas, one of My disciples. God gave each of you a measure of faith, But it is up to you to accept Me and grow your faith in Me. I am always here waiting for you, My lost sheep. The more you read My Word, the more you will grow faith in Me. You have to trust Me and My Word. I will not let you down."

Luke 15:1-5 - Tax collectors and other notorious sinners often came to listen to Jesus teach. This made the Pharisees and teachers of religious law complain that He was associating with such sinful people—even eating with them! So Jesus told them this story: "If a man has a hundred sheep and one of them gets lost, what will he do? Won't he leave the ninety-nine others in the wilderness and go to search for the one that is lost until he finds it? And when he has found it, he will joyfully carry it home on his shoulders...."

Luke 24:36 - And just as they were telling about it, Jesus Himself was suddenly standing there among them. "Peace be with you," He said.

John 20:24-29 - One of the twelve disciples, Thomas (nicknamed the Twin), was not with the others when Jesus came. They told him, "We have seen the Lord!" But he replied, "I won't believe it unless I see the nail wounds in His hands, put my fingers into them, and place my hand into the wound in His side." Eight days later the disciples were together again, and this time Thomas was with them. The doors were locked; But suddenly, as before, Jesus was standing among them. "Peace be with you," He said. Then He said to Thomas, "Put your finger here, and look at My hands. Put your hand into the wound in My side. Don't be faithless any longer. Believe!"

Romans 10:17 - *So faith comes from hearing, that is, hearing the Good News about Christ.*

Romans 12:3 - *Because of the privilege and authority God has given me, I give each of you this warning; Don't think you are better than you really are. Be honest in your evaluation of yourselves, measuring yourselves by the faith God has given us.*

I've felt led to share one more thing with you. The following are words I speak over my life. I don't always speak these daily, But sometimes I do them several days in a row. I have written these declarations over the last ten years of my life at various times...as I was led. I have them listed with Scripture to back my chosen words up.

His Word tells us to speak things as though they were and these are the declarations I speak over myself, my life. You should make yourself a list...and I don't mind if you use mine to start your own. I started doing this after I read a book by Joel Osteen about speaking declarations over yourself. God wants to pour blessings over you, But you have to do your part. Open the door to Him in prayer. Expect and receive.

As it is written...is what Jesus said to Satan. So use God's Word to speak truth over yourself.

Declarations I Speak Over Myself

My youth is renewed as my mouth is satisfied with good things. Psalm 103:5

I don't worry about having everything I need today or tomorrow. My trust is in You as I seek Your Kingdom and Your Righteousness. Matthew 6:33

I give my burdens to You, Jesus, and I rest as You carry all of them as I lay them at Your feet and leave them in Your more than capable hands. Thank You Jesus! Matthew 11:28

Everything I pray to You, I know will be answered...even though sometimes Your answer is no. I believe and receive answered prayers from You. Mark 11:24

I forgive everyone who sins against me so I can continue to live in Your peace as You answer my prayers! Mark 11:25

I am blessed and surrounded by Your love. Thank You God! Psalm 5:12

Lord, You are my rock, my fortress, and my Savior. I am surrounded by Your shield of protection and rest in Your safety. Psalm 18:2

Lord, You are my shelter. You alone are my refuge and my place of safety. I trust You to rescue me from every trap that comes my way and heal me from all deadly disease. You are my shelter, my rest, and my refuge. Thank You for loving me! Psalm 91

You, Lord God, forgive all my sins—heal all my diseases—redeem me—and cover me with Your loving kindness. Thank You, Lord! Psalm 103:3-4

I am prosperous with a hope and a future. Jeremiah 29:11

I am blessed. I am covered in Your favor, Lord God. I am more than a conqueror. Victory is mine! Romans 8:37

Your grace and peace cover me. 2 Peter 1:2

Blessings from You keep coming my way! Thank You Lord. Deuteronomy 28:2

What I do and wherever I go as I follow Your lead, I will be blessed. Deuteronomy 28:6

As I continue to read Your Word and follow Your way, You will help me be strong and courageous, and get through any trouble that comes my way. Thank You Lord. Joshua 1:7-9

As I live pure and righteous through the blood of Jesus, You keep coming to my aid. Thank You Lord! Job 8:6-7

You have shown me the path of life You have chosen for me. And as I stay on it, You will continue to fill me with joy and eternal pleasures at Your right hand! Psalm 16:11

Thank You Jesus for being my shepherd and leading me in Your ways. Your goodness and love following me always, every day. Thank You, Lord! Psalm 23:6

You are my strength Lord God. I fear no one! Psalm 27:1

My delight is in You and Your Word and Your plans for me. Thank you for giving me the desires of my heart. Psalm 37:4

Thank You for today...You made it! I am rejoicing and living a glad filled life! Psalm 118:24

You know the plans You have given me in writing, and I know You will fulfill them. I love You Lord. Psalm 138:8

Because I honored my mom and dad...and still do...You will give me a long life. Exodus 20:12

I commit my writing to You Lord God, and I know I will be successful. Proverbs 16:3

Thank You for helping me guard my mouth and what comes out of it, so You can continue to bless me daily. I love You Lord! Proverbs 21:23

My trust is in You. You are strong and protect me in times of trouble. Thank You Lord! Nahum 1:7

I do not worry about my tomorrows. They will have enough trouble. But I know You have me today! Matthew 6:33-34

When I pray and ask something that I know is in agreement with Your will, I thank You right away, then every day until it comes, I continue to thank You for my answered prayer. You are so faithful! Matthew 7:7

I am blessed with a rich and satisfying life. Thank You Lord! John 10:10

Thank You for the blessings and the rewards, I receive from You daily. I love You Lord, and love that You love me. Thank You Lord! Hebrews 11:6

I am healed by Your stripes Jesus. Your suffering, Your ripped and torn body paid the price for me, Jesus. Thank You! Isaiah 53:5

Your grace and peace are multiplied to me. Thank You, Lord. 2 Peter 1:2

Your favor, God, surrounds me as like a shield. Psalm 5:12

I do not fear, for You God are my shield and great rewarder. Thank You for blessing me in abundance. Genesis 15:1

I am more than a conqueror through You, Jesus. You love me. Romans 8:37

I have the mind of Christ. 1 Corinthians 2:16

I have the power of life and death in my tongue—so I choose to watch what I say. Help me Lord to always speak good over every one. Proverbs 18:21

Thank You for the Holy Spirit that lives in me and produces love, joy, peace, patience, kindness, goodness, faithfulness, gentleness, and self-control in me. Help me to always listen to the Holy Spirit in me. Galatians 5:22-23

REMEMBER...

When your flesh tells you that you don't deserve any of these wonderful blessings God wants to pour out on you, point to Jesus Christ - Your Savior - who suffered, bled and died so that all of you who believes are qualified for all of God's blessings because He said so. God wants to give you the best of everything!!!! But you have to believe and receive it...and keep focused on Him, in Him, trusting Him, resting on Him and His Word.

JESUS IS YOUR RIGHTEOUSNESS, your qualification, your sanctification!

Jesus defeated death, defeated sickness, defeated poverty. Through Him you'll live eternally on the new earth in the new heaven...and right now on this old earth all these blessings can be yours. Just trust in Him. Rest in Him. Know that Jesus is your qualification. You are the righteousness of God in Christ.

1 Corinthians 1:30 - God has united you with Christ Jesus. For our benefit God made Him to be wisdom itself. Christ made us right with God; He made us pure and holy, and He freed us from sin.

Scripture in But God Says...:

Old Testament:

Genesis———————————— 1:27-28a

Exodus————————— 15:2

20:17

33:14

Numbers——————— 6:24-26

Deuteronomy ————— 28:2

28:6

31:6

31:8

Joshua ———————— 1:8

` 1:9

1 Samuel———————— 16:7

Nehemiah——————— 8:10

Job————————————— 8:6-7

Psalm——————————— 5:12

16:8

16:11

18:2

20:4

23:1-2

23:6

27:1

27:14

28:7

21:23
22:6
23:4
24:16
Ecclesiastes————————— 6:9
Isaiah————————————— 30:18
41:10
46:4
51:12
54:13
55:8-9
64:6
Jeremiah—————————- 1:5a
1:7-8
17:5 - 8
17:9
17:14
29:11
30:17
33:3
Lamentations—————— 3:22-23
Daniel———————————— 9:21
Nahum ——————————— 1:7
Zephaniah————————— 3:17
Haggai ——————————- 2:7b-9
Malachi———————————- 3:6a
3:10
New Testament:
Matthew———————— 5:43-44
6:19-21
6:24
6:25-26

John——————————— 1:16
2:11
3:16-17
4:23-24
5:2
6:63
8:7
10:3,6,7
10:10
10:27-28
12:49
14:13-14
14:15-17
14:21
15:4
15:5
15:7
15:9
15:12
15:16
16:33
17:22-23
Acts——————————— 2:17
Romans ——————————— 2:1-2
3:10
3:23
4:5
4:20-21
5:8
5:11
5:15
5:17

2:10

3:20

4:26b-27

4:32

5:16-17

6:17

29b-30

Philippians——————————— 2:3

2:4

2:12-16

2:13

2:14-16

4:4-9

4:6

4:13

4:19

Colossians——————————— 1:13-14

1:22-23

3:12

3:23

1 Thessalonians—————————- 3:13

4:11-12

2 Thessalonians—————————- 3:2

3:13

1 Timothy ——————————— 5:3

5:5

6: 6&10

6:12

6:17

2 Timothy——————————————- 1:7

Hebrews——————————————— 1:2

3:6

Books by Deborah Lynne

Non-fiction:
Guidance from The Light
Blessings from God
But God Says...
Samantha Cain Mysteries:
Be Not Afraid
Testimony of Innocence
The Truth Revealed
Against Her Will
Stand-alone mystery/suspense:
Crime in The Big Easy
Hidden Secrets
Passion from the Heart
Coming in 2022, a second book for Taylor and John from PFTH
Romance:
Second Chances
All in God's Time
Grace, a Gift of Love
Young Adult Fiction:
Chasing The Lights
Listen Closely (coming in 2022, book 2 of the Cooper Parks
Adventures)

Bayou Secrets - a compilation of 3 of Lynne's mystery novels

About the Author

Deborah Lynne, mother of three, grandmother of five, is blessed to share her love for God through her writings in her fiction as well as her non-fiction. When Lynne started writing 33 years ago, she thought God had called her only to write fiction and share His love for us through it. A few years ago He encouraged her to write her first non-fiction, ***Guidance from The Light***, a one-year devotion.

This book is filled with Scripture God shared with her through a sad period in her life...the loss of her husband after almost 43 years of marriage. For two years she stayed deep in the Word. Then during her third year of loss, God led her to write the book, ***Guidance from The Light***, released in 2017. Two years later, she was led to write a second non-fiction, ***Blessings from God***. This book, too, is based on what God's Word Says. Again, its contents were encouraged by God. He loves us and wants to bless us...and wants us to know this. It was released in June 2019.

That same year, 2019, she had three new fiction novels (thoughts, ideas and working titles) she thought she was supposed to write, But He kept nudging her to first share the third non-fiction book He wants her to write. Deborah wants to please God and do as God Says, But like Moses, she sometimes feels she's not the right one...But then she's reminded — God knows best. He's called her for a reason, and she realizes He has a reason for ***But God Says...*** to come out before any more fiction is released...and this is it.

Deborah is a mother, a grandmother, an ex-secretary, retired dispatcher, and widow who God has chosen to share His love and His presence, with others, and she is proud to do it. So as she alters 'a little' what she used to say to everyone who would listen, she now Says — **Some** of my books are fiction, some non-fiction, But God is real in every one of them.

So she hopes you enjoyed and dug deep into the Word as you read her latest ***But God Says....*** She loves sharing Him with you.

Website - author-deborahlynne.com[1]

At present, her fiction is available in eBook form for $.99 each download on most eBook readers. Her non-fiction in eBook form is free on most eBook readers. All of her novels, fiction and non-fiction are available in book form at various prices through various venues. Recently, one book was released in audio form, ***Crime in The Big Easy***. She hopes more will follow.

---

1.   http://author-deborahlynne.com

www.ingramcontent.com/pod-product-compliance
Lightning Source LLC
Chambersburg PA
CBHW051210160726
47994CB00002B/547